Becker Professional Education, a global leader in professional education, has been developing study materials for ACCA for more than 20 years, and thousands of candidates studying for the ACCA Qualification have succeeded in their professional examinations through its Platinum and Gold ALP training centers in Central and Eastern Europe and Central Asia.*

Becker Professional Education has also been awarded ACCA Approved Content Provider Status for materials for the Diploma in International Financial Reporting (DipIFR).

Nearly half a million professionals have advanced their careers through Becker Professional Education's courses. Throughout its more than 50-year history, Becker has earned a strong track record of student success through world-class teaching, curriculum and learning tools.

We provide a single destination for individuals and companies in need of global accounting certifications and continuing professional education.

*Platinum – Moscow, Russia and Kiev, Ukraine. Gold – Almaty, Kazakhstan

Becker Professional Education's ACCA Study Materials

All of Becker's materials are authored by experienced ACCA lecturers and are used in the delivery of classroom courses.

Study System: Gives complete coverage of the syllabus with a focus on learning outcomes. It is designed to be used both t and as part of integrated study. It also includes the ACCA Syllabus and Study Guide, exam advice and commentaries and Bank containing practice questions relating to each topic covered.

Revision Question Bank: Exam style and standard questions together with comprehensive answers to support and prepa ir exams. The Revision Question Bank also includes past examination questions (updated where relevant), model answers and ns and tutorial notes.

Revision Essentials*: A condensed, easy-to-use aid to revision containing essential technical content and exam guidance

*Revision Essentials are substantially derived from content reviewed by ACCA's examining team.

Substantially derived from content reviewed by ACCA's examining team

ACCA

PAPER P4
ADVANCED FINANCIAL MANAGEMENT

REVISION ESSENTIALS
For Examinations to June 2016

©2015 DeVry/Becker Educational Development Corp. All rights reserved.

No responsibility for loss occasioned to any person acting or refraining from action as a result of any material in this publication can be accepted by the author, editor or publisher.

This training material has been published and prepared by Becker Professional Development International Limited.

16 Elmtree Road
Teddington
TW11 8ST
United Kingdom.

ISBN: 978-1-78566-136-5

Copyright ©2015 DeVry/Becker Educational Development Corp. All rights reserved.

All rights reserved. No part of this training material may be translated, reprinted or reproduced or utilised in any form either in whole or in part or by any electronic, mechanical or other means, now known or hereafter invented, including photocopying and recording, or in any information storage and retrieval system. Request for permission or further information should be addressed to the Permissions Department, DeVry/Becker Educational Development Corp.

For more information about any of Becker's materials, please visit our website at www.becker-atc.com or email acca@becker.com.

©2015 DeVry/Becker Educational Development Corp. All rights reserved.

CONTENTS

	Page
Syllabus	(iii)
Approach to examining	(iv)
Explanation of formulae sheet	(v)
Core topics	(ix)
Role of financial strategy	0101
Security valuation and the cost of capital	0201
Weighted average cost of capital and gearing	0301
Portfolio theory and CAPM	0401
Basic investment appraisal	0501
Advanced investment appraisal	0601
Business Valuation	0701
Mergers and acquisitions	0801
Corporate reconstruction and re-organisation	0901
Equity issues	1001
Debt issues	1101
Dividend policy	1201
Options	1301
Foreign exchange risk management	1401
Interest rate risk management	1501
The economic environment for multinationals	1601

CONTENTS

	Page
International operations	1701
Financial statement analysis	1801
Additional reading	1901
Examiner's article – Securitisation and tranching	2001
Article – Conditional probability	2101
Article – Integrated Reporting	2201
Article – Management and shareholder myopia	2301
Examiner's article – Interest rates, bond and swap valuation	2401
Article – Black Scholes model	2501
Article – Merton model	2601
Examiner's article – Risk management	2701
Article – How lenders set their rates	2801
Article – Modified Internal Rate of Return	2901
Article – Share buybacks	3001
Article – A question of values	3101
Examiner's report – December 2014	3201
Analysis of past exams	3301
Exam technique	3401

CAUTION: These notes offer guidance on key issues.
Reliance on these alone is insufficient to pass the examination.

Aim

To apply relevant knowledge, skills and exercise professional judgement as expected of a senior financial executive or advisor, in taking financial management decisions.

Main capabilities

- ✓ Explain the role and responsibility of the senior financial executive or advisor in meeting conflicting needs of stakeholders
- ✓ Evaluate the impact of macro-economics and recognise the role of international financial institutions in the financial management of multinationals
- ✓ Evaluate potential investment decisions and assess their financial and strategic consequences, both domestically and internationally
- ✓ Assess and plan acquisitions and mergers as an alternative growth strategy
- ✓ Evaluate and advise on alternative corporate re-organisation strategies
- ✓ Apply and evaluate alternative advanced treasury and risk management techniques
- ✓ Identify and assess the potential impact of emerging issues in finance and financial management.

Rationale

The syllabus starts by exploring the role and responsibility of a senior executive in meeting competing needs of stakeholders then moves on to assess the impact of the economic environment on multinationals.

The syllabus then examines investment and financing decisions, with the emphasis moving towards the strategic consequences of making such decisions in a domestic, as well as international, context.

Candidates are then expected to develop further advisory skills in planning strategic acquisitions and mergers and corporate re-organisations.

The next part of the syllabus covers the role of a treasury function in large complex corporate structures. It re-examines, in the broadest sense, the existence of risk in business and the sophisticated strategies which are employed in order to manage such risks. This builds on what candidates would have covered in the F9 *Financial Management* syllabus and P1 *Professional Accountant* syllabus.

The syllabus finishes by examining the impact of emerging issues in finance.

APPROACH TO EXAMINING

Format of the examination

The examination will be a three hour paper in two sections:

Section A: 1 compulsory question to total 50 marks
Section B: Choice of 2 from 3 questions,
each 25 marks

Section A will contain a compulsory question comprising 50 marks. This will cover significant issues relevant to the senior financial manager or advisor and will be set in the form of a short case study or scenario. The requirements of the section A question will demand comprehensive understanding of issues from across the syllabus.

The question in section A will contain a mix of computational and discursive elements. In part or whole of the question candidates will be expected to provide answers in a specified form (e.g. a short report or board memorandum) reflecting the professional level of the paper.

In section B candidates will be asked to answer two from three questions, each comprising 25 marks. Section B questions are designed to provide a more focused test of the syllabus. Questions will normally contain a mix of discursive and computational elements but may also be wholly discursive or evaluative where computations are already provided.

15 minutes for reading and planning is given at the start if the examination. During this time candidates may make notes on the question paper but may not write in the answer booklet.

Candidates will be provided with a formulae sheet as well as present value, annuity and standard normal distribution tables.

Candidates are advised to bring a scientific calculator.

©2015 DeVry/Becker Educational Development Corp. All rights reserved.

EXPLANATION OF FORMULAE SHEET

Modigliani and Miller Proposition 2 (with tax)

$$k_e = k_e^i + (1 - T)(k_e^i - k_d)\frac{V_d}{V_e}$$

This formula for the cost of equity is from M&M's model of capital structure in a world with corporation tax.

k_e = cost of equity geared
k_e^i = cost of equity ungeared
T = corporate tax rate
k_d = cost of debt (pre-tax)
V_d = total market value of debt
V_e = total market value of equity

Capital Asset Pricing Model

$$E(r_i) = R_f + \beta_i[E(r_m) - R_f]$$

This is the formula for CAPM. Input an asset beta to obtain the cost of equity ungeared, an equity beta will give the cost of equity geared.

$E(r_i)$ = expected return on an investment
R_f = risk-free interest rate
β_i = beta of the investment (i.e. level of systematic/market risk)
$E(r_m)$ = expected return on the market portfolio

Asset beta formula

$$\beta_a = \left[\frac{V_e}{(V_e + V_d(1-T))}\beta_e\right] + \left[\frac{V_d(1-T)}{(V_e + V_d(1-T))}\beta_d\right]$$

This is the formula for switching between an asset beta and equity beta.

β_a = asset beta
β_e = equity beta
β_d = beta of debt (usually assumed to be zero)

The Growth Model

$$Po = \frac{D_0(1+g)}{(r_e - g)}$$

This is the dividend valuation model which can be used to value ordinary shares in a growing company.

Po = today's ex-div share price
Do = most recent dividend
g = forecast average annual growth rate in dividends
r_e = required return of equity investors (i.e. cost of equity geared)

EXPLANATION OF FORMULAE SHEET

Gordon's growth approximation

$$g = br_e$$

A model for forecasting the growth rate as required for the dividend valuation model.

b = retention ratio (i.e. the proportion of annual profit reinvested back into the business)

r_e *= return on equity*

Weighted average cost of capital

$$WACC = \left[\frac{V_e}{V_e + V_d} \right] k_e + \left[\frac{V_d}{V_e + V_d} \right] k_d (1 - T)$$

This is the formula most commonly used to estimate the weighted average cost of capital

k_e *= cost of equity geared*

k_d *= cost of debt (pre-tax)*

Fisher formula

$$(1 + i) = (1 + r)(1 + h)$$

The relationship between the nominal discount rate, real discount rate and the inflation rate.

i = nominal discount rate
r = real discount rate
h = inflation rate

Purchasing power parity and interest rate parity

$$S_1 = S_0 \times \frac{(1 + h_c)}{(1 + h_b)} \qquad F_0 = S_0 \times \frac{(1 + i_c)}{(1 + i_b)}$$

Purchasing power parity claims that the spot exchange rate will change due to different inflation levels in different countries. Interest rate parity claims that the forward exchange rate reflects the difference in interest rates between two countries.

S_1 *= the forecast spot exchange rate*
S_0 *= today's spot exchange rate*
h_b *= the domestic inflation rate*
h_c *= the overseas inflation rate*
F_0 *= the forward exchange rate*
i_b *= the domestic interest rate*
i_c *= the overseas interest rate*

©2015 DeVry/Becker Educational Development Corp. All rights reserved.

EXPLANATION OF FORMULAE SHEET

Modified Internal Rate of Return

$$MIRR = \left[\frac{PV_R}{PV_I}\right]^{\frac{1}{n}} (1 + r_e) - 1$$

MIRR is the rate of return on a project assuming that its cash flows are reinvested at the firm's hurdle rate.

PV_R = present value of the project's returns

PV_I = present value of the investment outlay

n = number of years

r_e = reinvestment rate (i.e. cost of capital)

The Black Scholes Option Pricing Model

$$c = P_a N(d_1) - P_e N(d_2) e^{-rt}$$

Where:

$$d_1 = \frac{\ln(P_a/P_e) + (r + 0.5s^2)t}{s\sqrt{t}}$$

$$d_2 = d_1 - s\sqrt{t}$$

These formulae can be used to calculate the price (i.e. premium of a European call option). Details on how to use them can be found in a later section of these notes.

c = price of call option

P_a = price of the underlying asset

$N(d_1)$ = probability that a normal distribution is less than d_1 standard deviations above the mean

P_e = exercise price/strike price

r = annual risk free interest rate

t = time to expiry (in years)

s = annual standard deviation of the underlying asset's returns

e = the exponential constant

$\ln$ = the natural log (log to the base e)

EXPLANATION OF FORMULAE SHEET

The Put Call Parity relationship

$$p = c - P_a + P_e e^{-rt}$$

This formula can be used to convert the price of a call option (from the Black Scholes model) to the price of a put option (p).

Present value and annuity tables

These are also provided in the examination (not reproduced here).

Standard normal distribution table

This is also provided in the examination (not reproduced here).

This table can be used to calculate $N(d_i)$, the cumulative normal distribution functions needed for the Black-Scholes model of option pricing. If $d_i > 0$, add $0 \cdot 5$ to the relevant number above. If $d_i < 0$, subtract the relevant number above from $0 \cdot 5$.

©2015 DeVry/Becker Educational Development Corp. All rights reserved.

CORE TOPICS

Role and responsibility towards stakeholders

- Role and responsibility of senior financial executive/advisor ☐
- Financial strategy formulation ☐
- Conflicting stakeholder interests ☐
- Ethical issues in financial management ☐
- Environmental issues and integrated reporting ☐

Economic environment for multinationals

- Management of international trade and finance ☐
- Strategic business and financial planning for multinationals ☐

Advanced investment appraisal

- DCF techniques and free cash flows ☐
- Application of options pricing theory in investment decisions and valuation ☐
- Impact of financing on investment decisions and adjusted present value ☐
- Valuation and the use of free cash flows ☐
- International investment and financing decisions ☐

Mergers and acquisitions

- M&As versus other growth strategies ☐
- Valuation for M&As ☐
- Regulatory framework and processes ☐
- Financing M&As ☐

Corporate reconstruction and re-organisation

- Financial reconstruction ☐
- Business re-organisation ☐

CORE TOPICS

Tick when completed

Treasury and advanced risk management techniques

✓ The role of the treasury function
in multinationals ☐

✓ Using financial derivatives to hedge
against foreign exchange risk ☐

✓ Using financial derivatives to hedge
against interest rate risk ☐

✓ Dividend policy in multinationals
and transfer pricing ☐

Emerging issues in finance and financial management

✓ Developments in world financial markets ☐

✓ Developments in international trade
and finance ☐

✓ Developments in Islamic finance ☐

1 ROLE OF THE SENIOR FINANCIAL EXECUTIVE

- ✓ To advise management on complex strategic financial management issues facing an organisation, both domestically and internationally.
- ✓ Key issues include financing, investing, dividends and risk management.

2 CORPORATE OBJECTIVES

2.1 Corporate Objectives in Practice

- ✓ In practice company directors often use profit maximisation as a proxy for shareholder wealth maximisation.
- ✓ Total profits could be increased by redeeming all the firm's debt (and hence eliminating interest expense from the income statement).
- ✗ However shareholders would then lose the benefit of relatively cheap debt finance (and the "tax shield" created by interest expense) and their wealth may actually fall.
- ✗ EPS growth is also not necessarily consistent with wealth maximisation.
- ✗ For example EPS will rise significantly during a share buy-back programme, while shareholder wealth would theoretically be unchanged.

2.2 Maximisation of Shareholders' Wealth

- ✓ In theory the overall financial objective should be maximisation of shareholder wealth.
- ✓ The change in shareholder wealth is measured by Total Shareholder Return (TSR) – the combination of capital gain/(loss) and dividend yield.

3 CONFLICTS OF INTEREST

3.1 Agency Theory

- ✓ Agency theory refers to relationships involving a principal and an agent.

3.2 Stakeholders

- ✓ Company directors are the agents of various "stakeholders" (e.g. banks, bondholders, suppliers, customers and potentially even society as a whole).

3.3 Directors and Shareholders

- ✓ The key stakeholder in the corporate sector is the ordinary shareholders.

- ✓ Unless the firm is closely-held (e.g. a family business) there will be a "divorce of ownership and control" which creates the key agency relationship.

3.4 Transaction Cost Theory

- ✓ When a firm contracts with external parties (e.g. suppliers) various "transaction costs" may be incurred:

  - ➤ in searching for the best contractor;
  - ➤ in negotiating the contract;
  - ➤ preparing and enforcing the agreement.

- ✓ Rational directors will attempt to minimise such transaction costs – for example via vertical integration (acquiring suppliers and distributors).

3.5 Agency costs

- ✘ There is a risk that the directors will arrange transactions for their personal benefit rather than for their shareholder's benefit – for example "empire building" via expensive conglomerate-style acquisitions.

- ✘ This is known as the "agency problem" and the resulting loss in potential shareholder wealth "agency costs".

4 CORPORATE GOVERNANCE

4.1 Definition

- ✓ Good corporate governance (e.g. having a board balanced between executives and independent non-executive directors) should ensure that agency costs are reduced to an acceptable level.

4.2 Corporate Governance Around the World

- ✓ UK Corporate Governance Code – based on Cadbury's "principles of good governance". Compliance is voluntary for companies listed on the London Stock Exchange

- ✓ USA – firms listed on a USA stock exchange (including their overseas subsidiaries) must comply with the detailed rules of the Sarbanes-Oxley Act.

- ✓ Germany – firms often have two boards:

  - (1) management board;
  - (2) supervisory board (comprising stakeholder representatives).

- ✓ Japan – firms often have three boards:

  - (1) monocratic;
  - (2) policy;
  - (3) functional.

5 ETHICS

5.1 Ethical Contexts for the Financial Executive

Main Components

- Integrity
- Credit to the profession
- Independent judgement
- Competence

Fundamental Responsibilities

- Compliance with:
  - laws
  - regulations
  - professional standards
  - ethical codes.

Relationship With the Profession

- Use ACCA designation with dignity.

Relationship With the Employer

- Inform employer of obligation to comply with the ACCA's *Code of Ethics and Conduct*.

Interaction With Clients

- Put the client's interest before one's own.

Compliance With Anti– Money-Laundering Legislation

- Report any suspicion that the proceeds if crime are being disguised as being from legitimate business activity.

International Aspects

- Specific issues could include:
  - use of transfer pricing to reduce global tax;
  - "facilitation payments" (e.g. to acquire mineral exploitation rights);
  - following relaxed overseas rules on labour rights and environmental damage.

5.2 Ethical Frameworks

- Rest's Model
- Albrecht's Ethical Development Model (EDM)
- The International Accounting Education Standard's Board (IAESB) Ethics Education Framework

5.3 Ethical Decision-Making Models

- American Accounting Association (AAA) model
- Tucker's 5-Question Model
- ACCA Ethical Conflict Resolution
- Institute of Business Ethics (IBE)

6 ENVIRONMENTAL ISSUES AND INTEGRATED REPORTING

6.1 Sustainability

✓ Organisations of all types are increasingly under pressure to reduce any adverse environmental impacts (e.g. achieving carbon-neutral status).

✓ In the corporate sector this does not necessarily conflict with shareholder wealth as consumers may be attracted to firm's which show Corporate Social Responsibility (CSR).

6.2 Triple Bottom Line Reporting (TBL)

✓ A sustainable business model must balance financial objectives with social and environmental performance.

✓ Reporting these three areas of performance can be achieved using the TBL approach.

6.3 The Carbon Trading Economy

✓ Carbon Credits – where the government allocates a quota of permitted carbon emissions to polluting firms.

✓ If a firm reduces its carbon emissions it can sell its surplus carbon credits to those making excess emissions.

6.4 Government Environment Agencies

✓ Environmental Agencies – can impose fines for illegal environmental damage.

6.5 Integrated Reporting <IR>

✓ The International Integrated Reporting Council (IIRC) has formulated an IR Framework that reflects developments in financial governance, management commentary and sustainability reporting.

✓ It requires organisations to publish material information about their strategy, governance, performance and prospects in a clear, concise and comparable format.

7 RISK MANAGEMENT

7.1 Should Risk Be Managed?

✓ If a firm's shareholders have a large proportion of their wealth invested in that firm (e.g. a family-owned firm) they are exposed to *total* risk – systematic and unsystematic.

✓ In this case corporate diversification and hedging *will* reduce the shareholders' risk.

- ✓ However in the case of a large firm listed on the stock exchange, where most shareholders are institutions (e.g. pension funds) investors will have already used personal portfolio diversification to eliminate major unsystematic risks (industry, currency, interest rate, commodity price).

- ✓ In this case corporate risk management cannot further reduce the shareholder's risks.

7.2 Conflicts Between Equity and Debt Investors

- ✗ Debt investors (banks and bond holders) tend to use "restrictive covenants" to force management to focus on low-risk projects.

- ✓ Equity investors, who have unlimited upside potential and limited liability for losses, may prefer management to undertake higher risk projects.

- ✓ It is the role of the senior financial executive to resolve such stakeholder conflicts by finding, and communicating, a compromise acceptable to all parties.

7.3 Types of Risk

- ✓ Business
- ✓ Financial
- ✓ Credit (default)
- ✓ Reputational
- ✓ Operational
- ✓ Fiscal
- ✓ Regulatory
- ✓ Project
- ✓ Commodity price
- ✓ Interest rate
- ✓ Currency

7.4 Risk Mitigation, Hedging and Diversification

- ✓ Risk mitigation – dealing with a potential risk before it materialises (e.g. obtaining advance regulatory approval for an acquisition or merger).

- ✓ Hedging – using internal and external methods of hedging currency, interest rate and commodity price risks.

- ✓ Diversification – reducing exposure to a specific business via either:

    - ➢ portfolio diversification by shareholders; or
    - ➢ conglomerate diversification at the corporate level.

1 CAPITAL MARKET EFFICIENCY

1.1 Introduction

✓ The Efficient Markets Hypothesis deals with the pricing efficiency of the capital markets (i.e. what information is included in the price of securities).

✓ The rise of "dark pool trading" (i.e. off-market private trading) may be a challenge to the pricing efficiency of public markets.

1.2 Efficient Market Hypothesis

✓ Weak form efficiency – share prices reflect historic data about the share.

✓ Semi-strong efficiency – prices reflect all publically available information about the firm.

✓ Strong form efficiency – prices reflect all information, including inside information.

✓ An efficient market, where bargains do not exist, only emerges if there is a lot of active trading on that market.

✗ However investors will only trade actively if they believe that bargains are available.

1.3 Implications for Financial Managers

✓ Modern markets display the semi-strong level of pricing efficiency.

✓ A company should therefore release all material information about its operations as soon as practical in order for its share price to reflect fair value.

✗ In such a market bargains will not exist and hence no quick gains should be expected from mergers and acquisitions.

2 DIVIDEND VALUATION MODEL

2.1 General Model

✓ If capital markets are perfect, the sale/purchase of any security will be a zero NPV transaction – bargains should not exist.

✓ Therefore the market value of a security = present value of its future cash flows discounted at investors' required return.

✓ Applying this to shares gives the dividend valuation model.

✓ Market value of a share = present value of future dividends discounted at shareholders' required return.

©2015 DeVry/Becker Educational Development Corp. All rights reserved.

2.2 Constant Dividend

- $Po = \dfrac{D}{r_e}$

Where:

Po = ex-div share price (most recent dividend just paid)
D = annual dividend per share
r_e = required return of shareholders

2.3 Constant Dividend Growth

- $P_O = \dfrac{D_O(1+g)}{(r_e - g)}$

Where:

Do = most recent dividend per share (just paid)
g = forecast annual growth rate in dividend per share

3 COST OF EQUITY

3.1 Shareholders' Required Rate of Return

- If the market price of a share is already known, then the dividend valuation model can be rearranged to imply the required return of shareholders.
- The required return of ordinary shareholders = the firm's cost of equity.

3.2 Dividend With Constant Growth

- $r_e = \dfrac{D_0(1+g)}{Po} + g$

3.3 Growth From Past Dividends

- If an exam question provides several years of historic dividend per share data then calculate the geometric average annual growth rate and assume this will continue in future.

3.4 Gordon's Growth Model

- $g = br_e$

where

b = proportion of profits reinvested back into the business (retention ratio)

r_e = return on equity, estimated using the ratio (profit after tax/shareholders' funds).

3.5 Cost of Preference Shares

- Preference dividends are a fixed % of the share's par value – a constant dividend per share with zero growth.
- $r_e = \dfrac{D}{Po}$

4 BOND VALUATION AND COST OF DEBT

4.1 Terminology

✓ Nominal value = par value = face value

✓ Coupon interest rate = fixed % on the nominal value

✓ Ex-int market price = market value of the bond where any accrued interest has just been paid

4.2 Irredeemable Bonds

Valuation of Irredeemable Bonds

✓ Future interest payments on an irredeemable (undated) bond are a perpetuity (with zero growth) hence:

$$\text{Bond price} = \frac{\text{Annual interest}}{\text{Required return}}$$

✓ Required return of bondholders = the firm's pre-tax cost of debt.

Cost of Irredeemable Bonds

✓ Pre-tax cost = current yield = annual coupon interest/ex-int market price

✓ Post-tax cost = current yield × (1–tax rate)

4.3 Redeemable Bonds*

Valuation of Redeemable Bonds

✓ Market value = present value of future interest and redemption price discounted at the bondholders' required return.

✓ The required return on a redeemable bond may be quoted as the bond's yield to maturity.

Cost of Redeemable Bonds

✓ Pre-tax cost = gross redemption yield (yield to maturity) = IRR of pre-tax cash flows (market price, coupon interest payments and redemption price).

✓ Post-tax cost = IRR of post-tax cash flows (interest is tax allowable, redemption is not).

4.4 Convertible Bonds

Valuation of Convertible Bonds

1. Forecast the expected conversion value (conversion ratio × forecast share price at conversion date).

2. Compare the forecast conversion value to the redemption price – a rational investor will choose the higher of the two options.

3. Market value = present value of future interest and the *higher* of:

   ➢ redemption price; and
   ➢ forecast conversion value.

Cost of Convertible Bonds

✓ Post-tax cost = IRR of:

   (i) market price
   (ii) post-tax coupon interest payments
   (iii) higher of conversion/redemption value.

4.5 Bank Loans

Valuation

✓ As bank loans are not traded assume the face value = market value (an accurate assumption for floating rate loans but not for fixed rate).

Cost

✓ The quoted interest rate on bank loans can be taken as the pre-tax cost.

✓ Post-tax cost = pre-tax cost × (1−tax rate)

4.6 Bond Duration

✓ Macaulay duration (years) = weighted average period of a bond's future cash flows, the weighting being the proportion of total present value generated in each year.

✓ Modified duration (%) = Macaulay duration/(1 + yield to maturity).

✓ Modified duration measures the (approximate) sensitivity of a bond's market value to a change in yield.

✗ However the true relationship is convex not linear.

5 TERM STRUCTURE OF INTEREST RATES

5.1 Yield Curve Theory

✓ The term structure of interest rates can be analysed by examining the "yield curve" – a graph plotting interest rates against various maturities of government debt.

✓ A "normal" yield curve slopes upwards with long-term debt being more expensive than short-term debt.

✓ An "inverse" yield curve slopes downwards with long-term debt being cheaper than short-term debt.

Various theories have been proposed to explain any yield curve profile:

Liquidity preference theory -

✓ if the government (or a company) wants to borrow for a longer period it must offer higher compensation to investors for deferring their liquidity.

Expectations Theory

✓ The yield curve reflects future interest rate expectations.

✓ Expectations of falling interest rates could cause an inverse yield curve.

Market Segmentation Theory

✓ Investors may have a "preferred habitat" on the yield curve.

✓ For example pensions fund managers may prefer to invest in long-term bonds (to match against the long-term liabilities of the pension fund). This would push up the market price of long-term bonds and hence drive down the yield, inverting the yield curve.

5.2 Deriving the Spot Yield Curve

✓ A "spot" interest rate refers to the rate that would apply if money borrowed today is to be repaid by a *single future sum.*

✓ The treasury spot yield curve could be directly observed if the government had issued *zero-coupon* debts of various maturities.

✓ A one-year treasury bill will be repaid by a single future sum and hence its yield to maturity = one-year spot.

✓ However medium and long0term treasuries will be repaid by a series of coupon payments in addition to the final redemption,

✓ Therefore medium and long-term spot rates cannot be directly observed but can be implied using "bootstrapping".

5.3 Valuing Corporate Bonds Using Spot Rates

✓ Treasury spot yield + corporate credit spread = corporate spot yield.

✓ Discount each future cash flow from the corporate bond at the respective corporate spot yield.

✓ Sum the present values = market price.

1 WEIGHTED AVERAGE COST OF CAPITAL

1.1 Calculation of WACC

- WACC is a *potential* discount rate for estimating project NPV

Published formula

$$WACC = \left[\frac{V_e}{V_e + V_d}\right]k_e + \left[\frac{V_d}{V_e + V_d}\right]k_d(1-T)$$

Where:

K_e = the cost of equity *geared* – the return required by ordinary shareholders to compensate them for the business risk and any financial risk they face

V_e = the total market value of equity

V_d = total market value of debt

K_d = pre-tax cost of debt

T = corporation tax rate.

1.2 Limitations

- The firm's existing WACC should only be used as a discount rate if:
  - the project would **not** change the firm's business risk; and
  - the project finance would **not** change the firm's capital structure.
- Difficult to estimate for unquoted firms.

2 EFFECTS OF GEARING

- Financial gearing refers to the proportion of debt in the firm's capital structure.
- Interest on debt is a fixed (committed) cost and increases the volatility of profits available to ordinary shareholders.
- This additional volatility is known as *financial risk* which leads to a rise in the cost of equity.
- At high levels of gearing the providers of debt will become concerned that the firm may default on the payment of interest and/or principal.
- This is *credit risk* which leads to a rise in the cost of debt.

3 TRADITIONAL VIEW OF CAPITAL STRUCTURE

✓ Per the traditional view the WACC initially falls due to the tax shield on debt.

✓ However the cost of equity starts to rise due to financial risk and potentially the cost of debt will rise due to credit risk.

✓ Therefore at some point the WACC will start to rise.

✓ This suggests there may be an optimal capital structure at which WACC is minimised.

✓ If the WACC is minimised then the NPV of projects is maximised and, in turn, shareholders' wealth.

4 MODIGLIANI AND MILLER'S THEORIES

4.1 Introduction

✓ Modigliani and Miller (MM) produced models based on assumptions that may not hold in practice.

✓ Assumptions include:

> perfect capital markets;
> no agency costs;
> no financial distress costs.

4.2 Theory without Tax

✓ MM proved that the WACC is independent of capital structure and hence this is sometimes referred to as "gearing irrelevance theory".

✓ Conclusion:

> there is **no** optimal capital structure; and
> a firm's value is only affected by its investment decisions and not by how it is financed.

4.3 Theory With Tax

✓ MM proved that as gearing rises the additional tax shield on debt will cause the WACC to continuously fall.

✓ The conclusion is that a firm should use as much debt as possible if it wants to maximise its overall market value.

Published formula

$$k_e = k_e^i + (1-T)(k_e^i - k_d)\frac{V_d}{V_e}$$

Where.

k_e = cost of equity *geared*
k_e^i = cost of equity *ungeared*
T = corporate tax rate
k_d = cost of debt (pre-tax)
V_d = total market value of debt
V_e = total market value of equity

4.4 Impact of Default Risk

✓ MM believed that default (credit) risk represents a transfer of part of the firm's business risk away from shareholders to the debt investors.

✓ Therefore while the cost of debt rises the cost of equity *falls*.

✗ This view is disputed as default risk is an additional class of risk as opposed to a segment of existing business risk.

4.5 Practical Considerations

✓ Financial distress costs – at high levels of debt the firm's customers may lose confidence in any guarantees attached to its products, employees may look for new jobs, suppliers may refuse to give credit.

✓ Quality of assets available as collateral – a firm with large holdings of property has higher debt capacity than a human resource firm.

✓ Personal tax effects – dividend income may be taxed at a different rate than interest income, distorting investor preference for equity and debt.

5 PECKING ORDER THEORY

5.1 Using Retained Earnings

✓ Internal equity finance = reinvested profit.

✓ Efficient working capital management is required to ensure that profits are quickly converted into cash available for reinvestment.

5.2 Preference for Internal Finance

✓ The economists Brealey and Myers found that company managers simply use the most convenient source) of financing for a project.

✓ This is known as "pecking order theory" and the hierarchy that emerged is:

   (i)   internal equity finance;

   (ii) debt;

   (iii) external equity.

6 AGENCY THEORY AND CAPITAL STRUCTURE

6.1 Agency Costs

✓ Directors are the agents of shareholders and there is a risk that the directors will fail to maximise shareholder wealth.

✓ Lost potential wealth = agency costs.

6.2 Impact of Gearing on Agency Costs

✓ Introducing debt may encourage the directors to improve the firm's financial control – *reducing* agency costs.

✘ However at high levels of gearing the debt contracts will include restrictive covenants (e.g. forcing the firm to reject risky but potentially attractive projects). This *increases* agency costs.

✓ There may be an optimal level of gearing in terms of minimising agency costs.

7 STATIC TRADE-OFF THEORY

✓ The use of increased debt creates a trade-off between:

➢ increased tax shield; and

➢ increased agency costs.

✓ An optimal capital structure may exist based on balancing these effects.

1 WHAT IS RISK?

1.1 Definition

- Risk = variability of returns

1.2 Measurement

- Standard deviation – measures the dispersion of an investment's returns around their mean value.

1.3 Investors and Risk

- Rational investors will attempt to reduce risk if there is no reduction in expected return.

2 PORTFOLIO THEORY

- The standard deviation of a portfolio's returns will almost always be less than the weighted average risk of its underlying investments.
- The only exception is if the investments are "perfectly positively correlated" – which is very rare in practice.
- Whilst calculations on portfolio theory are not examinable the concept of risk-reduction through diversification certainly is within the syllabus.

2.4 Systematic v Unsystematic Risk

- Most shares in listed firms are held by institutional investors (e.g. pension funds).
- Fund managers use diversification to reduce the risk of their portfolios.
- The type of risk that can be reduced, and potentially removed, is known as unsystematic risk.
- For example both transport companies and oil companies are affected by the oil price but in opposite directions – holding shares in *both* companies will hedge this specific (unsystematic) risk to some degree.
- Ultimately an investor could hold shares in *every* company listed in the stock market – the "market portfolio".
- ✗ Whilst the market portfolio contains zero unsystematic risk it is still rises/falls – this residual volatility is known as "systematic risk".

2.5 Implications for Financial Management

✗ If the firm's shareholders have personally used portfolio diversification then any *corporate* diversification (e.g. through conglomerate acquisitions) will *not* lead to any further risk reduction for its investors.

✓ If shareholders are diversified the firm should *specialise.*

3 CAPITAL ASSET PRICING MODEL

3.1 Measurement of Systematic Risk

✓ Beta factors measure the relative amount of systematic risk of a particular share.

3.2 Calculation of Beta

✓ Beta factors are calculated (by business schools and data agencies) through linear regression of the historic volatility of returns from a particular share compared to the market portfolio.

3.3 Interpretation of Beta

✓ Beta > 1 if a share is more volatile than the market
✓ Beta < 1 if a share is less volatile than the market
✓ Beta = 1 for the l stock market overall
✓ Beta = 0 for a risk-free investment

3.4 CAPM Formula

✓ $E(r_i) = R_f + \beta_i(E(r_m) - R_f)$

Where:

$E(r_i)$ = expected return on an investment
R_f = risk-free interest rate
β_i = beta of the investment
$E(r_m)$ = expected return on the market portfolio

✓ $(E(r_m) - R_f)$ is referred to as the "market risk premium".

3.5 Uses of CAPM

Investors

✓ The investor they can use CAPM to calculate the *required* return on a share to compensate for its level of systematic risk.

✓ If the investor forecasts that the *actual* return will be higher this would be a signal to buy the share.

Companies

✓ CAPM is an alternative to the dividend valuation model for estimating a company's cost of equity.

✓ To estimate the *ungeared* cost of equity (the required return to compensate for systematic business risk) an *asset beta* should be input into CAPM.

- ✓ To estimate the *geared* cost of equity (the required return to compensate for systematic business risk and financial risk) an *equity beta* should be input into CAPM.

3.6 Project-specific discount rates

- ✓ If a project would *change* the firm's business risk then a *project-specific* cost of equity is required.

Steps

1. Find the equity beta of a "proxy" company which already operates in our proposed project's area of business.
2. "De-gear" the proxy's equity beta down to an asset beta as we are only concerned about the proxy's business risk, not its financial risk.
3. "Re-gear" the asset beta to reflect *our* firm's capital structure. This gives an equity beta measures the project's business risk and our firm's financial risk.
4. Use CAPM to find the project-specific cost of equity, and ultimately, a project-specific WACC.

- ✓ Steps 2 & 3 are performed using the published formula:

$$\beta_a = \left[\frac{V_e}{(V_e + V_d(1-T))}\beta_e\right] + \left[\frac{V_d(1-T)}{(V_e + V_d(1-T))}\beta_d\right]$$

β_a = asset beta (ungeared beta)
β_e = equity beta (geared beta)
β_d = beta of corporate debt. Debt investors receive fixed contractual returns and hence the common assumption is $\beta_d = 0$.

3.7 Assumptions of CAPM

- ✓ Perfect markets.
- ✓ Investors have personally diversified away all unsystematic risk.
- ✓ There is a linear relationship between risk and required return.

3.8 Advantages

- ✓ CAPM is more flexible than the dividend-based model for calculating the cost of equity as CAPM can estimate project-specific discount rates.
- ✓ Unlike the dividend-based model CAPM can estimate the cost of equity of zero-dividend firms.

3.9 Limitations

✘ CAPM puts all its faith in beta factors – in practice a range of factors may influence required returns

✘ CAPM is a single-period model whereas company projects tend to be multi-period.

✘ Beta factors can only be calculated for listed firms and hence there may be a lack of data for firms in the "new economy".

4 ARBITRAGE PRICING THEORY (APT)

✓ APT is a multi-factor model which attempts to find a range of key factors that influence required returns.

✓ APT is not a practical model due its complexity – the returns on different shares are affected by different factors and hence a specific cost of equity formula would have to be developed for each firm.

1 NON-DCF METHODS OF INVESTMENT APPRAISAL

1.1 Purpose of Investment Appraisal

✓ Investment appraisal is used to make capital expenditure decisions.

1.2 Payback Period

✓ Payback period is the time taken for a project's operating cash flows to recover the initial cost of investment.

1.3 Return on Capital Employed (ROCE)

✓ ROCE is a relative (%) measure that compares the average operating profit of a project to the level of investment in that project.

✓ ROCE is also referred to as Accounting Rate of Return (ARR) or Return On Investment (ROI).

2 DISCOUNTED CASH FLOW TECHNIQUES

2.1 Time Value of Money

✓ The time value of money concept is based on the assumption that investors prefer to receive $1 today rather than $1 at some point in the future.

2.2 Discount Factors

Single Cash Flow

✓ Formula as published above the present value tables:

$$(1 + r)^{-n}$$

where r = discount rate
n = number of periods until payment

✓ The tables provide the discount factors for discount rates up to 20% and periods up to 15 years.

✓ These discount factors can be used to find the present value of a single future sum of money

✓ Present value = future value × discount factor

Annuities

✓ Formula as published at the top of the annuity tables:

$$\frac{1-(1+r)^{-n}}{r}$$

✓ The tables provide the annuity factors for discount rates up to 20% and periods up to 15 years.

✓ Present value of an annuity = annual cash flow × annuity factor.

BASIC INVESTMENT APPRAISAL

Perpetuities

✓ A perpetuity is an equal annual cash flow to infinity.

✓ Present value of a perpetuity = annual cash flow $\times \dfrac{1}{r}$

3 NET PRESENT VALUE (NPV)

3.1 Procedure

✓ Forecast the investing and operating cash flows from a project.

✓ Discount to present value using the firm's cost of capital.

✓ Sum the present values.

3.2 Meaning

✓ NPV gives the theoretical dollar change in the total market value of the firm's equity due to the project.

✓ NPV therefore estimates the absolute change in shareholder's wealth.

✓ A project should be undertaken if its NPV > \$0.

3.3 Cash Budget Pro Forma

✓ Whilst there is no unique pro-forma that will suit every exam scenario it is important to produce a clear and neat project cash flow forecast.

✓ Reference any complex calculations to separate workings.

3.4 Tabular Layout

✓ If there is an equal annual cash flow for several years (an annuity) it is more efficient to use an annuity factor rather than discount each year' cash flow individually.

4 INTERNAL RATE OF RETURN (IRR)

4.1 Definition

✓ IRR is the discount rate at which NPV = 0 and measures the annualised cash return over the life of an investment.

✓ A project should be accepted if its IRR > the firm's cost of capital.

4.2 Method

- ✓ Most company projects will not involve perpetuities or annuities but will have different operating cash flows in each year.

- ✓ In this case calculate the project's NPV at two chosen discount rates, then use linear interpolation to estimate the discount rate at which NPV = 0.

4.3 Unconventional Cash Flows

- ✓ Convention projects have an initial cash outflow (capital expenditure) followed by a series of (uneven) operating cash inflows, This cash flow structure changes direction just once and has one IRR.

- ✗ An unconventional cash flow structure is where the cash flows change direction more than once. In this case there is potentially more than one IRR (calculations would not be required on this during the examination).

4.4 NPV v IRR

- ✓ NPV is an absolute measure whereas IRR is a relative measure.

- ✓ NPV gives information about a project's scale and is reliable when choosing between mutually exclusive projects.

5 RELEVANT CASH FLOWS FOR DISCOUNTING

5.1 General Rule

- ✓ Relevant for DCF are investing cash flows and future, incremental, operating cash flows.

- ✓ Opportunity costs (e.g. lost contribution on existing products) are also relevant and should be shown as a cash outflow.

- ✗ Never deduct depreciation because it is not a cash flow.

- ✗ Never deduct interest expense as the discounting process itself deals with the cost of financing the project (the discount rate being the firm's weighted average cost of capital).

5.2 Tax System

Effect on Investment Appraisal

- ✓ Tax will be paid on the project's net revenues (revenues – operating costs).

- ✓ Tax may be saved on the investment through claiming tax-allowable depreciation.

Timing of Tax Cash Flows

- ✓ Check whether tax is paid in the same year as project returns or is paid "one year in arrears".

BASIC INVESTMENT APPRAISAL

Other Assumptions

✓ Assume the initial investment is made on the *first* day of an accounting year.

✓ No "tax exhaustion" – sufficient taxable profits exist to use tax allowances as soon as possible.

✓ Changes in the level of working capital has no tax effects.

Exam Approach

✓ Multiply each year's net revenues by the stated tax rate to find the tax to be paid.

✓ Produce a cross-referenced working for any tax savings on allowable depreciation. In the year of disposal calculate the tax saved on a balancing allowance or paid on a balancing charge.

5.3 Inflation

Real and Money (or Nominal) Interest Rates

✓ The published Fisher formula relates nominal interest rates, real interest rates and the general inflation rate:

(1 + nominal rate) = (1 + real rate) (1 + general inflation rate)

✓ In the context of project appraisal the Fisher formula can be used to switch between the firm's nominal and real cost of capital.

✓ Exam questions may refer to the nominal cost of capital as the "money" cost of capital.

General and Specific Inflation Rates

✓ A project's operating cash flows will not necessarily inflate at the general inflation rate in the economy.

✓ The new product's sales price may rise at a specific rate, labour costs will be affected by wage inflation and materials costs affected by their own inflation rate.

5.4 Cash Flow Forecasts

Money (or Nominal) Cash Flows

✓ The default approach is to forecast the project's operating cash flows in *nominal* terms – inflating each cash flow (revenues, labour costs, material costs, overheads) at its specific inflation rate.

Real Cash Flows

✓ Theoretically each year's total nominal cash flow could then be *deflated* at the *general* inflation rate to become a cash flow in *real* terms.

©2015 DeVry/Becker Educational Development Corp. All rights reserved.

5.5 Discounting

Money Method

- ✓ If cash flows have been expressed in nominal terms they should be discounted at the firm's nominal cost of capital.

Real Method

- ✓ If cash flows have been expressed in real terms they should be discounted at the firm's real cost of capital.
- ✓ Theoretically each method will result in the same NPV.

5.6 Working Capital

- ✓ An initial investment in working capital would be required – a cash outflow.
- ✓ If during the life of the project the level of working capital rises there will be further cash outflows, if the level falls then cash inflows.
- ✓ Note that is the *change* in the level of working capital that creates the cash flow.
- ✓ Default assumption is that working capital is "released" at the end of the final year – creating a cash inflow.
- ✓ Cross cast all working capital adjustments – they should net to zero.

6 IMPACT ON REPORTED FINANCIAL POSITION AND PERFORMANCE

6.1 Relevance

- ✓ The directors of a *listed* firm need to be aware of how investing and financing decisions may affect the published financial statements and key ratios.

6.2 Impact of the Project

- ✓ The asset will be capitalised in the statement of financial position,
- ✓ Depreciation expense will reduce reported profits.
- ✓ Over time accumulated depreciation will reduce the net book value of the asset.

6.3 Mode of Financing

Internal Equity Finance

- ✓ The decision to reinvest profits (rather than distribute as a dividend) will cause retained earnings to be higher and reported financial gearing to be lower.

BASIC INVESTMENT APPRAISAL

Debt Finance

- ✘ If the firm takes a bank loan or issued bonds this will increase the firm's reported financial gearing until the date the debt is repaid.

- ✓ If the asset is leased, and the lease is treated as a finance lease, this would also increase the firm's reported gearing. However the outstanding balance on the lease would amortise over its life, and hence reported gearing would progressively fall from its peak.

- ✓ If an operating lease is used this would not impact on reported financial gearing as operating leases are not brought onto the statement of financial position.

External Equity Finance

- ✓ Shareholders' funds will rise by the amount of finance raised and financial gearing will fall.

1 ADJUSTED PRESENT VALUE (APV)

1.1 Use

- Traditional NPV (using WACC) does not deal well with a project whose finance significantly changes the firm's capital structure.
- In this situation, it is preferable to use APV.

1.2 Approach

- "Base case NPV" = investing and operating cash flows, discounted at the *ungeared* cost of equity.
- Value of tax shield = tax savings on interest, discounted at the *pre-tax* cost of debt.
- "Side effects" – for example, subsidies and issue costs, discounted at rates reflecting the related risk.
- APV = Base case + tax shield +/- side effects

2 CAPITAL RATIONING

2.1 Terminology

- Capital rationing occurs when there is not enough finance (capital) available to undertake all available positive NPV projects.
- If a projects is "divisible" then any proportion of that project can be undertaken, if "non-divisible" then the project, if accepted, must be undertaken at full scale.
- If projects are "mutually exclusive" then one or the other can be undertaken, but not both.
- "Hard" rationing – where potential equity and/or debt investors are not prepared to inject new capital into the business – perhaps due to high perceived risk.
- "Soft" – where management imposes internal limits on the funds available for investment (e.g. to avoid marginal projects from being accepted).

2.2 Single-Period Capital Rationing

- Divisible projects – Profitability indexes" should be used to rank the projects and identify those which should take priority.

- Profitability index = $\dfrac{\text{NPV}}{\text{Initial investment}}$

- Non-divisible projects – the optimal investment plan can only be found by comparing the total NPV produced by each possible combination of projects.

ADVANCED INVESTMENT APPRAISAL

✓ Mutually exclusive projects – create "sets", each containing one of the mutually exclusive projects, then choose the set that produces the highest total NPV.

2.3 Multi-Period Capital Rationing

✓ Multi-period capital rationing occurs where investment funds are restricted for more than one year.

✓ A linear programming model would be required.

✓ Exam questions may require the formulation of a linear programming model or the interpretation its output.

3 MODIFIED INTERNAL RATE OF RETURN

3.1 Limitations of Traditional IRR

1. As a relative (%) measure it gives no indication of a project's scale

2. A project with unconventional cash flows may have multiple IRRs.

3. Unrealistic reinvestment assumption – IRR would only be achieved if the project's surplus cash flows can be reinvested at the IRR itself.

✓ Modified Internal Rate of Return (MIRR) can deal with limitations 2 & 3.

3.2 Meaning of MIRR

✓ MIRR is the rate of return on a project assuming that its cash flows are reinvested at the firm's "hurdle rate".

✓ Hurdle rate = required rate of return on reinvestment = the firm's cost of capital.

3.3 Published Formula

$$MIRR = \left[\frac{PV_R}{PV_I} \right]^{\frac{1}{n}} (1 + r_e) - 1$$

PV_R = present value of the project's returns
PV_I = present value of the investment outlay
n = number of years
r_e = reinvestment rate

4 ANALYSING PROJECT LIQUIDITY

4.1 Traditional Measures

✓ Payback period – the number of years for the operating cash flows from a project to recover the initial investment.

✓ Discounted payback – the number of years for the *present value* of operating cash flows to recover the initial investment.

4.2 Project Duration

- ✓ Project duration = weighted average period of a project's future cash flows, the weighting being the proportion of total present value generated in each year.

5 ANALYSING PROJECT RISK

5.1 Probability Analysis

- ✓ Use historic data to forecast the probability of future outcomes (e.g. demand being high or low).

5.2 Expected Values

- ✓ An expected value is the weighted average of possible outcomes, weightings being the probability of each outcome.
- ✗ An expected value would only be achieved in practice if the decision was repeated many times, whereas company projects usually only occur once.

5.3 Standard Deviation

- ✓ Measures the dispersion of possible outcomes around the expected value.

5.4 Sensitivity Analysis

Method

- ✓ Sensitivity analysis estimates by how much key variables can change before a project's NPV falls to zero.
- ✓ Sensitivity for individual cash flows (revenues, labour costs etc.) can be expressed as a %:

$$\text{Sensitivity} = \frac{\text{Project NPV}}{\text{PV of individual cash flow}} \times 100$$

Advantages of Sensitivity Analysis

- ✓ Identifies the project's critical success factors.

Limitations of Sensitivity Analysis

- ✗ Does not indicate the *probability* that a variable will change significantly.
- ✗ Ignores inter-relationships between variables.

5.5 Monte Carlo Simulation

Designing a Monte Carlo Simulation

- ✓ State the key variables and any inter-relationships between them.

- ✓ Attach random numbers to the possible values of each variable.

- ✓ Pick sets of random numbers to simulate possible outcomes from the project.

Outputs From Monte Carlo Simulation

- ✓ Provided not only the project's mean NPV (the average of all possible outcomes) but also the *dispersion* (standard deviation) of possible outcomes around that mean.

Advantages of Monte Carlo

- ✓ Simulation models can be used to map all the possible outcomes from a project.

Limitations of Monte Carlo

- ✗ Monte Carlo simulations are only as good as the assumptions and estimates used.

- ✗ Complex and require powerful computers and specialised software.

5.6 Value at Risk (VaR)

- ✓ VaR estimates the potential loss of NPV below its expected value, at a given level of probability.

- ✓ Calculation of VaR requires use of the published normal distribution tables.

5.7 Stress Testing

- ✓ Foresting the outcome for a project (or an entire firm) under the worst-case scenario.

- ✓ May be a statutory requirement in the banking sector to ensure survival of a financial crisis.

5.8 Managing Risk

- ✓ Choosing projects with relatively quick payback period or low duration.

- ✓ Choosing projects will relatively low standard deviation of returns.

- ✓ Searching for potential early exit routes in case a project performs badly (e.g. selling the assets to a third party).

5.9 Project Monitoring and Control

- ✓ A suitable project manager should be appointed to ensure that costs do not spiral out of control and that any construction timescales are met.

5.10 Post-Completion Audit (PCA)

- ✓ At the end of each project a PCA should be undertaken to ensure any mistakes are not repeated in future.

1 BUSINESS VALUATION

1.1 Reasons For

✓ Estimating the share price for an IPO.

✓ Valuing a potential acquisition target.

1.2 Nature

✓ Equity valuation is an art not a science.

✓ Different methods, and different assumptions, will give different valuations.

2 ASSET-BASED VALUATION METHODS

2.1 Net Book Value (NBV)

✓ Assets – liabilities = equity

✓ The book value of equity is readily available from the published statement of financial position.

✗ However the statement of financial position may already be out of date.

✗ Heavily dependent on accounting policies (e.g. revaluations are permitted under IFRS whereas US GAAP only uses historic costs).

✗ Many key assets may be unrecorded (e.g. value of the brand, human capital and internally-generated goodwill).

2.2 Net Realisable Value (NRV)

✓ Asset values are written down to liquidation values before deducting liabilities.

✗ Only relevant if the owners are planning to break-up the business.

2.3 Replacement Cost

✓ Each asset is restated to the cost of buying it on the market, then liabilities deducted.

✓ Estimates how much it would cost to replicate the company rather than buying it as a whole.

✗ However market prices may not be available for some assets.

2.4 "Book Value-Plus"

✓ This method attempts to include the value of intangible assets not recorded on the statement of financial position.

✓ Value of equity = Book value of net assets + (annual profit × multiplier).

✗ The multiplier is highly subjective.

3 RELATIVE VALUATION MODELS

3.1 Price/Earnings Ratios

- ✓ To value the equity of an unquoted firm apply the average price/earnings ratio (share price/earnings per share) of quoted firms in the same business sector.
- ✓ Value of equity = profit after tax × sector P/E ratio.
- ✗ However the sector P/E may not reflect the specific risk profile or growth prospects of the firm being valued.

3.2 Earnings Yield

- ✓ Earnings yield = (earnings per share/share price) × 100
- ✓ Earnings yield is simply the reciprocal of a P/E ratio.
- ✓ Value of equity = profit after tax/earnings yield.

3.3 Dividend Yield

- ✓ Dividend yield = (dividend per share/share price) × 100
- ✓ Value of an unquoted firm's share = DPS/sector dividend yield
- ✗ The major limitation of dividend yield is that it does not take into account potential growth.

3.4 Tobin's Q

$$\frac{\text{Market value of equity}}{\text{Replacement cost of net assets}}$$

- ✓ If Tobin's Q >1 this indicates that the firm (or the entire stock market) may be overvalued.
- ✗ Difficult to estimate the replacement cost of assets.

3.5 Market to Book Ratio

$$\frac{\text{Market value of equity}}{\text{Book value of net assets}}$$

- ✓ To value the equity of an unquoted firm apply the average market-to-book ratio of "proxy" quoted firms in the same business sector.
- ✓ Value of equity = book value of net assets × sector price-to-book ratio.
- ✗ The proxy firms may themselves be under or overvalued.

4 DIVIDEND VALUATION MODEL

4.1 Ordinary Shares

✓ The value of a share should equal the present value of its future dividend stream.

Published growth model formula

$$P_O = \frac{D_O(1+g)}{(r_e - g)}$$

Where:

Po = Ex-div share price

r_e = required return of equity investors (the company's geared cost of equity)

Do = the most recent dividend per share (just paid)

g = forecast annual average growth rate in dividend per share

✓ For a mature company it may be acceptable to use the historical dividend growth rate but an alternative is Gordon's growth approximation:

✓ $g = br_e$

b = proportion of profits reinvested back into the business (retention ratio)

r_e = return on equity (profit after tax/shareholders' funds)

✗ Whilst the dividend valuation model is theoretically solid it requires careful forecasting of growth rates and a CAPM-based estimate of the cost of equity.

4.2 Preference Shares

✓ Preference dividends are a perpetuity (with zero growth) hence:

$$Po = \frac{D}{re}$$

5 FREE CASH FLOW MODELS

5.1 Introduction

- If the required data is available free cash flow valuation is considered superior methodology compared to asset-based or relative valuation methods.

5.2 Free Cash Flow to Equity (FCFE)

- FCFE = dividend capacity = cash flow available to ordinary shareholders.
- FCFE is stated *after* interest expense and should be discounted at the geared cost of equity.
- Present value of FCFE = value of equity.
- Theoretically equivalent to the dividend valuation model except that FCFE *can* deal with zero-dividend firms (which use their dividend capacity to build cash reserves rather than make distributions).

5.3 Forecasting Growth of FCFE

- Gordon's growth approximation can be applied:

    $g = br_e$

    b = proportion of surplus cash reinvested in the business

    r_e = expected return on equity (from CAPM)

5.4 Free Cash Flow to the Firm (FCFF)

- FCFF = cash flow available to *all* providers of long-term finance.
- FCFF is stated *before* interest expense and should be discounted at the WACC.
- Present value of FCFF = value of the firm's assets.
- Value of equity = value of assets − value of liabilities.

6 VALUE ADDED METHODS

6.1 Economic Value Added (EVA™)

- EVA™ = post-tax operating profit − (capital employed × WACC)

6.2 Market Value Added (MVA)

- MVA = present value of forecast EVA™
- Book value of capital employed + MVA = market value of capital employed.
- Market value of equity = market value of capital employed − market value of debt.

7 HIGH GROWTH START-UPS

✓ Start-ups are notoriously difficult to value due to uncertainties about the future of the business.

✓ The "Chepakovich Model" is an attempt to make reasonable forecasts of revenues and costs for a high growth firm (which may initially be loss-making).

8 PRACTICAL POINTS

8.1 Marketability

✘ The shares of unquoted firms are not traded on the stock exchange and, everything else being equal, would have a lower value than listed shares.

✓ Therefore the P/E ratio of listed firms should be adjusted downwards before being used to value an unquoted firm.

8.2 Information Sources and Availability

✘ Valuation of an unquoted company can also be difficult due to a lack of publically available information about the firm.

8.3 Market Imperfections and Pricing Anomalies

✓ Even quoted share prices are not necessarily a reliable indicator of the share's true value.

✓ For example share prices often fall at the end of December as investors sell some holdings to take capital gains within tax-free limits. Prices then rise again at the beginning of January as investors buy back the shares.

8.4 Market Capitalisation

✓ If a firm is considering making a bid to takeover a listed firm then the target's market capitalisation will be relevant as a guide to the minimum acceptable offer.

✓ Market capitalisation = market price per share × number of issued ordinary shares

8.5 Behavioural Finance

✘ Research into behavioural finance shows that market prices are often significantly above/below the true value of shares.

✓ A good example is the "irrational exuberance" that led to the "dot com bubble" on the NASDAQ exchange in the 1990's and, more recently, the rise in the Shanghai stock market.

MERGERS AND ACQUISITIONS

1 NATURE OF MERGERS AND ACQUISITIONS

1.1 Organic Growth v External Growth

- Many company directors view mergers and acquisitions (M&As) as the key to maintaining a high level of growth for the business.
- Whilst organic growth may be slower it avoids the risk of potentially complex and expensive acquisitions.

1.2 Criteria for Selecting Target

- Strategic fit
- Price
- Potential synergies
- Compatibility of systems and culture
- Risk of regulatory intervention

1.3 Strategic classification

- Horizontal integration – buying a competitor.
- Vertical integration forwards/backwards – buying a distributor/supplier.
- Conglomerate – buying a firm in an unrelated industry.

1.4 Advantages and Disadvantages

- ✓ Rapid business expansion.
- ✓ Potentially under-valued target.
- ✓ Access to new technology and/or markets.
- ✗ High transaction costs.
- ✗ High "control premium" may be expected by the target firm's shareholders.

1.5 Difference Between an Acquisition and a Merger*

- For exam purposes it is two names for the same topic.
- In practice the deal may be viewed as a merger if the firms involved are of similar size and the transaction is executed via a share-for-share exchange.

1.6 Synergy

- It is possible that the combined value of the new group will be higher than the sum of each company's existing value.
- The additional value created may be partly due to synergy benefits.

1.7 Sources of Synergy

✓ Cost synergies – increased power of over suppliers, sharing activities such as R&D.

✓ Revenue synergies – increased market power, cross-selling opportunities.

✓ Financial synergies – reduced volatility of group cash flows may lead to an improved credit rating.

1.8 Impact on Shareholders

✓ It is important to evaluate the potential gains/losses for both groups of shareholders – those of the acquirer and the target firm.

✓ The target firm's shareholders will almost certainly enjoy a gain due to the premium paid for their shares.

✓ Any gain for the acquiring shareholders depends largely on whether the value of synergy > control premium.

1.9 Risk of Overvaluation

✗ The acquiring firm's director are at risk of overvaluing the target firm due to:

  ➢ irrational exuberance – over optimistic projections;
  ➢ confirmation bias – choosing the valuation method that appears to justify their intended bid price.

1.10 High Failure Rate

✗ There is significant empirical evidence to suggest that many real-life M&As actually *destroy* wealth for the acquiring firm's shareholders.

✗ Either the premium paid for control is too high and/or the synergy benefits of combining the companies never become a reality.

✗ In fact synergy may turn out to be *negative* (e.g. due to a cultural conflict between the organisations or IT systems that cannot be integrated).

2 VALUATION OF ACQUISITIONS

2.1 General Principles

✓ If data is available then a range of valuation techniques may be used (asset-based, use of multiples, dividend-based, discounted cash flow models, EVA™).

✓ However it is discounted cash flow models which are fundamentally superior.

2.2 Valuation Classification

✓ Type I – target firm is in the same business as the acquirer and the proposed method of financing the bid does not disturb the acquirer's capital structure.

- ✓ Type II – target firm is in the same business as the acquirer but the proposed method of financing the bid *does* disturb the acquirer's capital structure.
- ✓ Type III – target firm is in a *different* business. If the acquirer's capital structure also changes then it is still classed type III.

2.3 Valuation of Type I Acquisitions

- ✓ Value target firm as a stand-alone entity (taking into account synergy effects and transaction costs).

2.4 Valuation of Type II Acquisitions

- ✓ Adjusted Present Value may be appropriate to deal with the change in capital structure:

1. Forecast the target's operating cash flows (including synergy) and discount at its ungeared cost of equity.
2. Forecast the tax shield on the target's debt *and* any debt raised by the acquirer to finance the bid – discount at the group's expected pre-tax cost of debt.
3. Calculate the present value of transaction costs (discounted at the risk-free rate).
4. 1 + 2 − 3 = value of target firm's assets.
5. Value of target's equity = value of target's assets − value of target's debt.

2.5 Valuation of Type III Acquisitions

1. Calculate the weighted average asset beta of the acquirer and target (weight using best available data – ideally by the relative value of each firm's assets).
2. Re-gear the combined asset beta to a combined equity beta reflecting the group's expected level of financial gearing.
3. Input the combined equity beta into CAPM to calculate the combined cost of equity.
4. Input the cost of equity into combined WACC reflecting the group's expected level of financial gearing and post-acquisition cost of debt.
5. Find the present value of combined operating cash flows (acquirer + target + synergy) at the combined WACC. This gives the combined value of the firms' assets.
6. Combined value of equity = combined value of assets − combined value of debt
7. Value of target's equity = combined value of equity − acquirer's existing value of equity.

MERGERS AND ACQUISITIONS

3 METHODS OF FINANCING AN ACQUISITION

3.1 Options Available

✓ M&As can be financed like any other project – per pecking order theory hierarchy is (i) internal equity (ii) issuing debt (iii) issuing equity.

✓ However with M&As equity can be issued to the target's firms shareholders in a share-for-share exchange (share swap).

3.2 Internal equity (cash reserves)

✓ Gives certainty as cash has a fixed value.

✓ Avoids issue costs.

✗ Paying cash for the target's shares may create an instant capital gains tax liability for its shareholders.

3.3 Issuing debt (to finance a cash bid)

✓ Additional tax shield for the acquirer.

✗ Additional financial risk and potentially credit risk.

3.4 Share swap

✓ Gives ongoing equity participation for the target firm's shareholders.

✗ Creates an uncertain gain for the target's shareholders as difficult to forecast the acquirer's post-acquisition share price.

4 STRATEGY AND TACTICS

4.1 Strategy

✓ Estimate maximum bid price to be offered.

✓ Mode of payment – cash, share swap, or a combination of both (mixed mode).

✓ Tactics – "Dawn raid" or "formal offer".

4.2 Dawn Raid

✓ As soon as the stock market opens and without any warning the "predator" buys as many shares as possible in the target firm.

✓ The objective is to acquire these shares before the target's directors can launch any defence.

✓ Therefore a hostile raid can be cheaper than approaching the target firm's directors in advance.

©2015 DeVry/Becker Educational Development Corp. All rights reserved.

- There is a regulatory limit to the maximum proportion of shares that can be acquired this way – in the UK the limit is 30%. Once this limit is reached the predator must make a formal offer for the remaining 70% of the shares.

4.3 Formal Offer

- Where the acquirer approaches the target's board who must then:
  - inform their shareholders of the offer;
  - work in their shareholders' best interests.
- In the UK the "City Code" regulates the process.

4.4 Competition Law

- In the UK the Competition and Markets Authority (CMA) uses 25% (product/service) market share as a signal of potential unfair market influence – the CMA may intervene in M&As that would break this limit.

4.5 Merger and Acquisition Activity in Different Countries

- UK and USA – active in M&As as listed firms tend to have a large "free float" as most shares are held by institutional investors.
- Germany – less M&As as commercial banks tend to be major shareholders and are reluctant to give up control.
- Japan and South Korea – less M&As due to cross-shareholdings between companies and their suppliers/distributors.

4.6 Regulatory Devices in Takeovers

- "Squeeze out" – once 90% (per UK law) of the target's shares have been acquired the predator can force the remaining shareholders to sell.
- "Breakthrough provisions" – where the target firm has a class of shares with disproportionate voting rights or blocks on their transfer, the acquirer can use the law to remove such mechanisms.

5 DEFENCES AGAINST A BID

5.1 Hostile Bids

✓ If the directors of a (potential) target believe that a change in ownership would not be in the firm's best interest then various defences against hostile bids may be used.

5.2 Defences Before a Bid Is Made

✓ Poison pills – requiring debt to be immediately repaid on a change in ownership.

✓ Golden parachutes – large compensation packages for loss of office.

✓ Crown jewels – disposing of assets that are attractive to predators.

✓ Cross-shareholdings with suppliers or distributors.

✓ "Golden shares" with large voting rights.

5.3 Defences After a Bid Is Made

✓ White Knight – inviting the directors of a "friendly" firm to start a bidding war with the predator.

✓ Pac Man – making a bid for the predator.

✓ Publicity

6 POST-MERGER MONITORING

✓ Care must be taken to ensure that expected synergy becomes real (e.g. through integrating IT and transferring best practice throughout the group).

1 ESTIMATING CREDIT RISK

1.1 Introduction

- Credit risk = default risk = the probability the firm cannot meet the interest and/or principal payments on its debt.

1.2 Ratings Agencies

- Agencies (e.g. Fitch) use their own models for analysing credit risk, focusing on factors such as industry risk, country risk, earnings protection and quality of management.

1.3 Structural Models

- Analyse either:
    - the level and volatility of assets and hence the risk they will fall to the level of liabilities; or
    - the level and volatility of cash and hence the risk it will fall to zero.

2 CAPITAL RECONSTRUCTIONS

2.1 Background

- If management or stakeholders identify a significant risk of bankruptcy then steps should be taken to avoid this.
- Company law in many countries allows some form of capital reconstruction.

2.2 Types of Capital Reconstruction

- Simple – writing off a debit balance on retained earnings (representing accumulated losses). Purpose is to allow dividends to be paid as soon as the firm becomes profitable, making it easier to attract new equity finance.
- Complex – fundamentally changes the position of various stakeholders (e.g. a debt-to-equity swap in which debt is written off in exchange for a significant shareholding).

2.3 Analysing a Complex Reconstruction

(1) Forecast the position of each stakeholder if the firm is liquidated (secured creditors would be repaid first, ordinary shareholders would probably receive nothing).

(2) Forecast the position of each stakeholder if the proposed reconstruction is undertaken.

(3) Forecast the cash flows on reconstruction.

2.4 Factors Affecting Success of Scheme

- Would each stakeholder be in a better position post-reconstruction compared to liquidation?

- ✓ Does the proposal also provide sufficient finance to recapitalise the firm? Note that a debt-to-equity swap does not itself raise any finance.

- ✓ Does the firm have a viable "turnaround" plan to move it back into profitability?

- ✗ In 2006 over half the seats on flights within the US were with airlines under "Chapter 11 bankruptcy protection" and many seats were empty due to over-capacity.

3 DIVESTMENT

3.1 Reasons for Divestment

- ✓ Even a healthy company may wish to restructure its operations (e.g. to focus on core activities or to separately list potentially undervalued business segments).

3.2 Divestment Strategies

- ✓ "Sell-off" – of a business segment (e.g. if it is considered non-core and/or or to raise cash to repay debt).

- ✓ De-merger – existing shareholders have old share cancelled and replaced with two new shares; one in each of the newly separated businesses. Value can potentially be unlocked by making each business segment more transparent, hence removing the "conglomerate discount".

- ✓ "Spin-off" – a non-core activity is transferred into a newly set-up company whose shares are issued pro-rata to the existing shareholders. Like a demerger no cash is raised, in fact cash would fall due to the transaction costs.

4 MANAGEMENT BUYOUTS

- ✓ Management Buy Out (MBO) – where the existing management team buys all, or part of, the company they work for.

- ✓ An MBO may be used to achieve a "sell-off" of a subsidiary or division.

- ✗ Management are unlikely to have sufficient personal finance available for the buyout, hence MBOs are often highly "levered" with large amounts of debt involved.

- ✓ Potential financiers include venture capitalists who would also like some equity participation (e.g. through investing convertible debt).

- ✓ Management Buy In (MBI) – where an external management team buy a business and replace the existing management team.

1 STOCK EXCHANGE ADMISSION

1.1 The Stock Exchange

- ✓ Primary role – providing a market for companies to issue new securities to raise finance.
- ✓ Secondary role – to allow investors to trade in existing securities.

1.2 Reasons for Wanting a Listing

Advantages of a Listing

- ✓ The stock exchange offers a large potential source of finance for the firm.
- ✓ Increased reputation.
- ✓ Provides an "exit route" for existing shareholders.

Disadvantages of a Listing

- ✗ Public share issue is a complex and expensive process.
- ✗ Ongoing costs – increased reporting requirements, cost of compliance with corporate governance codes.
- ✗ Increased public scrutiny of the firm's ethical and environmental performance.
- ✗ Risk of hostile takeover.

1.3 Regulatory Requirements of Major Stock Exchanges

- ✓ London Stock Exchange (LSE) Main Market – at least a 25% of shares must be made available to the public ("free float").
- ✓ The LSE discourages (but does not ban) the use of "dual-class shares" (where a small group of insiders hold a special class of share giving them large voting rights).
- ✓ New York Stock Exchange (NYSE) – $40m minimum free float and *no* restriction on dual-class shares (for this reason the Chinese online retailer Alibaba chose to list on NYSE rather than Honk Kong which bans dual-class shares).

2 METHODS OF ISSUING SHARES

2.1 Listed Firms

- ✓ Rights issue – existing shareholders are offered new shares, at a discounted price, in proportion to their existing holding.
- ✓ Placement – if existing shareholders agree to "waive" their pre-emptive rights then the firm, via a merchant bank, can "place" blocks of shares with new investors.

2.2 Unquoted Firms

✓ As above – rights issues or (private) placements.

✓ Initial Public Offering (IPO) – becoming a listed firm and issuing new shares to the general public.

3 IPO METHODS

✓ Offer for Subscription – the company sells shares directly to the public.

✓ Offer for Sale – the company sells shares to an intermediary who then sells to the public.

✓ Fixed price – where the IPO price is set in advance.

✓ Dutch Auction – where potential investors are asked to submit tenders stating the price they are prepared to pay. The IPO price is then set at a level to ensure all shares are sold.

✓ Role of sponsor – a sponsor must make written confirmations concerning the directors' responsibilities and reports presented.

4 ALTERNATIVES TO THE MAIN MARKET

4.1 Listing on the Alternative Investment Market (AIM)

✓ AIM is part of the London Stock Exchange.

✓ It has more relaxed listing rules than the Main Market (e.g. no requirement for a 25% minimum "free float").

✓ It may be appropriate for a Small or Medium Sized Enterprise (SME) to make an IPO.

4.2 Trade Sale to Another Company

✓ An alternative exit route for a firm's founders may be a sale of the firm to a competitor.

4.3 Unquoted Equity Finance

✓ Venture capital funds – provide "seed" finance for new start-ups and growth finance for more established firms.

✓ Private equity funds – often want a controlling stake.

✓ Business angels – retired entrepreneurs who provide finance and business experience, but only for the most outstanding applicant.

✓ Crowdfunding – where large numbers of individuals invest a small amount each in return for shares or "rewards" such as discounts. See https://www.kickstarter.com

1 DOMESTIC DEBT MARKETS

1.1 Financial Intermediaries

- ✓ Financial intermediaries are "middlemen" who bring together lenders and borrowers – examples include commercial banks, investment banks, pension funds and insurance companies.

1.2 Role of Financial Intermediaries

- ✓ Aggregation
- ✓ Maturity transformation
- ✓ Risk diversification
- ✓ Providing liquidity
- ✓ Offering derivatives.

1.3 The Money Market

- ✓ Provides short-term finance (up to one year) to companies and the government.

2 SHORT-TERM FINANCE

2.1 Bank Overdraft

- ✓ Flexible and interest is only paid on the exact amount of finance required.
- ✗ Overdraft interest rates tend to be high and overdrafts are repayable on demand.

2.2 Trade Credit

- ✓ May represent interest-free credit.
- ✗ Taking extended credit may result in lost discounts or even refusal by the supplier to provide more materials.

2.3 Bills of Exchange

- ✓ Often used in international trade, a bill of exchange is a document signed by a customer who promises to pay a fixed sum of money on a fixed date.
- ✓ Rather than wait for the customer to pay the exporter can immediately sell the bill to a bank (at a discount to face value).

2.4 Commercial Paper

- ✓ A money market instrument issued by a company at a discount to face value to be repaid at face value.
- ✗ Only available to firms will very good credit ratings.

3 MEDIUM-TERM FINANCE

3.1 Bank Loans

- ✓ May be secured or unsecured.
- ✓ Interest carries a tax shield.

3.2 Leasing

✓ The firm may benefit from the bulk-buying power of the lessor.

✓ Lease payments should be tax allowable.

✓ If the lease is classified as "operating", as opposed to "financing" then no debt will be recorded in the statement of financial position.

3.3 Sale and Leaseback

✓ If a firm has significant property and wishes to raise finance then sale and leaseback may be an option.

✗ Once the property is sold the firm will not benefit from any further rises in property values.

4 LONG-TERM DEBT FINANCE

4.1 Preference Shares

✓ Preference shares are, in substance, debt:

> ➤ pay a fixed committed dividend in priority to any ordinary dividend;

> ➤ rank ahead of ordinary shares on liquidation.

✓ Preference shareholders face lower risk than ordinary shareholders and require lower returns.

✗ There is no tax shield on preference dividends.

4.2 Bonds

✓ An example of "financial disintermediation" – rather than taking a bank loan the firm can issue bonds and borrow directly from investors.

✓ Bondholders take even lower risks than preference shareholders as interest must be paid before preference dividends and bonds rank ahead of preference shares on liquidation.

✓ Bonds can be secured or unsecured. The security can be specific assets (a fixed charge) or a class of assets (a floating charge). If default occurs the assets are sold to repay the bond.

4.3 Deep Discount Bonds

✓ Deep discount bonds are bonds issued at a discount to face value but redeemable at face value on maturity.

✓ The annual "coupon" interest rate will be relatively low compared to bonds issued at face value.

4.4 Zero-Coupon Bonds

- ✓ Issued at a large discount to face value and pay zero annual interest.

4.5 Convertibles

- ✓ Convertibles are bonds, or preference shares, which can be converted into ordinary shares.
- ✓ For an investor, a convertible is a relatively low-risk debt investment combined with the opportunity to make high returns on conversion to ordinary shares.
- ✓ For an issuer, convertibles require a lower rate of interest than on non-convertible bonds (or a lower dividend than would be required for non-convertible preference shares).

4.6 Warrants

- ✓ Warrants are share options attached to a debt issue (the debt itself is *not* convertible).
- ✓ Issuing debt with options attached allows a relatively low interest rate to be offered.

4.7 Securitisation

- ✓ Securitisation is the process of transforming an illiquid asset into cash.
- ✓ Banks themselves often use securitisation by selling their mortgage loan books in the form of "mortgage-backed securities" or, in the case of sub-prime mortgages, "collateralised debt obligations".
- ✓ A firm with rental income could promise to divert this into a special purposes vehicle (SPV) which issues bonds secured on this future cash inflow. The SPV is "ring-fenced" so that it cannot be touched if the firm itself later becomes insolvent.
- ✓ Securitisation is therefore also a credit enhancement technique as the SPV would achieve a high credit rating and issue bonds at low interest rates.

4.8 Recent Developments in Debt Finance

- ✓ Peer-To-Peer (P2P) lending – where individuals (or other firms) directly lend money to firms.
- ✓ "Shadow banking" – where financial institutions (e.g. insurance companies) directly lend money to firms.
- ✓ Private debt funds – investment funds that lend directly to *unquoted* firms.

5 EUROMARKETS

5.1 Definition

✓ Euromarkets are the banking and financial markets located *outside* of the country which issues the currency.

✓ A currency which has left its country of issue is "offshore" and therefore outside of the issuing central bank's regulation.

5.2 Eurocurrency Market

✓ Short to medium-term bank deposits and loans (mostly less than one year).

✓ Borrowers are governments and "blue-chip" companies with high credit ratings.

✓ Floating interest rates.

5.3 Eurocredit Market

✓ Medium to long-term floating rate bank loans.

✓ High credit rating required.

✓ Large loans are provided by syndicates of banks.

5.4 Euronote Market

✓ A variety of short to medium-term debt instruments issued directly by blue-chip companies into the Euromarkets.

5.5 Eurobond Market

✓ Long-term debt issued directly into the Euromarkets.

✓ Usually underwritten by a syndicate of international banks.

✓ Fixed or floating interest rates.

✓ Do not usually require security.

✓ Used by multi-nationals to raise very large amounts of finance relatively quickly.

✓ A large proportion of Eurobond issues are "swap driven" in that they are combined with either interest rate or currency swaps.

1 DOMESTIC DIVIDEND POLICY

1.1 Stable Dividend

- ✓ Listed firms will avoid surprising the market and tend to announce a stable, or stable rise in dividend per share.

1.2 Constant Payout Ratio

- ✓ The firm distributes a constant % of profits as dividend.
- ✓ Dividends will therefore rise/fall with profits.

1.3 Residual Dividend Policy

- ✓ Dividend = Cash generated from operations – investment in positive NPV projects
- ✗ The resulting dividend pattern is likely to be volatile.

1.4 Clientele Theory

- ✓ A firm's historic dividend policy may have attracted particular groups of investors.
- ✗ A change in policy may annoy key investors who could sell their shareholdings which would reduce the share price.

1.5 Bird-in-the-Hand Theory

- ✓ Investors may prefer the risk-free nature of a dividend today as opposed to an uncertain capital gain if the firm reinvests the cash back into the business.

1.6 Dividend Irrelevance Theory

- ✓ Modigliani Miller proved mathematically that, under perfect market assumptions, the *pattern* of dividend payments should have no impact on the share price.

1.7 Dividend Valuation Model

- ✓ Theoretically the market value of a share = present value of expected future dividend stream.

1.8 Share Buyback Programmes

- ✓ The firm uses surplus cash to repurchase its own shares.
- ✓ Popular with investors if tax on capital gains is less than the tax rate on dividend income.
- ✗ In practice share buybacks are often driven by the directors' desire for large bonuses linked to growth in earnings per share.

1.9 Special Dividends

✓ The firm uses surplus cash to pay a "one off" bonus dividend.

1.10 Scrip Dividends

✓ Where the firm offers investors a choice of a traditional cash dividend or new shares in lieu of cash.

✓ The purpose is to retain more cash within the firm for reinvestment.

1.11 Zero Dividend

✓ Common with high-growth firms that wish to reinvest all surplus cash back into the business.

✓ Popular with investors if tax on capital gains is less than the tax rate on dividend income.

1.12 Practical Considerations

Legal Constraints

✗ A firm can only pay a dividend from "distributable reserves" which are usually the realised profits.

Liquidity Requirements

✗ Paying high dividends can lead to company liquidity problems later if unexpected expenses arise.

Shareholder Expectations

✓ Firms must carefully manage shareholder (and analyst) expectations regarding dividends – this is particularly important for listed firms.

Signalling

✓ Unless the firm is closely held (e.g. a family business) investors will not have full information about a firm's operations and prospects.

✓ Therefore dividend announcements are viewed as key signals of company strength or weakness.

2 DIVIDEND CAPACITY

2.1 Definition

- ✓ Dividend capacity is the amount of cash generated which is available for potentially paying a dividend.
- ✓ Dividend capacity = Free Cash Flow to Equity (FCFE).

2.2 Uses of dividend capacity

- ✓ Dividend capacity can be used to:
  - ➤ pay a dividend;
  - ➤ finance a share buyback programme; or
  - ➤ build cash reserves.

2.3 Multinational Corporations

- ✓ Dividend capacity = domestic FCFE + dividends received from overseas subsidiaries.
- ✓ Dividends received from overseas will be influenced by the host government's policies on currency convertibility, withholding taxes and even blocks on dividends.

3 INTERNATIONAL DIVIDEND POLICY

3.1 Tax Planning

- ✓ Global tax may be minimised by setting up an offshore "dividend mixer company" between the parent and overseas subsidiaries.
- ✓ This entity collects dividends from subsidiaries and then pays them together to the parent.
- ✓ By mixing dividends from higher and lower tax jurisdictions into a single source the parent can maximise claims under double-tax treaties – but may not comply with ethical standards or be awarded the "fair tax" mark.

3.2 Management of Blocked Remittances

- ✘ If an overseas government imposes restrictions on the payment of dividends to an overseas parent company then the group must consider other methods of repatriating cash.
- ✓ Alternatives include the use of interest payments from the subsidiary to parent, royalties or licence fees, management charges and transfer pricing.

1 NATURE AND USES OF OPTIONS

1.1 Terminology

✓ The holder of an option has the right, but not the obligation, to buy (if *calls*) or sell (if *puts*) an underlying asset at a fixed price (the *strike or exercise price*) on (if *European* style) or before (if *American* style) an agreed date (the *expiry date*).

✓ The cost of acquire an option is the *premium* that must be paid,

1.2 Exchange Traded Options

✓ Some options are traded through a formal derivatives market.

✓ The derivatives market is very active and displays high "price transparency" – quoted premiums should reflect fair value.

1.3 Over-The-Counter (OTC) Options

✓ OTC options are provided directly by a bank to its client.

✓ OTC options can be customised to the client's exact requirements.

1.4 Uses of Options

✓ Options can be used either for speculative purposes or for hedging.

✓ The corporate financial manager should consider the use of options for risk management, not risk taking.

2 ELEMENTS OF OPTION VALUE

2.1 Definitions

✓ In perfect markets the value of an option = the price of the option = the premium.

✓ An option's value has two main components – intrinsic value and time value.

2.2 Intrinsic Value of an Option

✓ Intrinsic value = theoretical gain for the holder if the option is exercised today.

✓ Found by comparing the strike price to today's market price of the underlying asset.

✓ Intrinsic value can be zero or positive – but not negative (as the holder of an option does not have the obligation to exercise it).

2.3 Time Value of an Option

Components of Time Value

✓ An option's time value relates to the possibility of the intrinsic value being higher in future. Time value has three elements:

1. Time to expiry – options which are far from expiry date are more valuable than options close to expiry.
2. Volatility of underlying asset – options on volatile assets are more valuable, and hence expensive, than options on stable assets.
3. Level of interest rates – the holder of a *call* can delay payment for the underlying asset until the option's expiry date. If interest rates in the economy rise the present value of this payment falls, this increasing the value of the option. The opposite holds for puts.

3 BLACK-SCHOLES OPTION PRICING MODEL

3.1 Formulae

$$c = P_a N(d_1) - P_e N(d_2)e^{-rt}$$

Where:

$$d_1 = \frac{\ln(P_a/P_e) + (r + 0.5s^2)t}{s\sqrt{t}}$$

$$d_2 = d_1 - s\sqrt{t}$$

c = price of *call* option

P_a = market price of the underlying asset

$N(d_1)$ = probability that a normal distribution is less than d_1 standard deviations above the mean

P_e = exercise price (strike price)

r = annual risk-free interest rate (as a decimal)

t = time to expiry (in years)

s = annual standard deviation of the underlying asset's returns (as a decimal)

e = the exponential constant

$\ln$ = the natural log (log to the base e)

3.2 Assumptions and Limitations of the Model

Assumptions

✓ The option is a European style call option.
✓ Perfect markets.
✓ Returns on the underlying asset follow the normal distribution.

Limitations

✗ Less accurate for valuing American style options
✗ In practice the returns from assets do not necessarily follow the normal distribution (e.g. share prices tend to exhibit a "fat tails" distribution, with large rises/falls occurring more frequently than predicted by the normal distribution).

3.3 Put-Call Parity

$$p = c - P_a + P_e e^{-rt}$$

Where p = price of a put option.

3.4 Options on Dividend-Paying Shares

✓ If a dividend will be paid between today and the expiry date of the option then the share price would fall from cum-div to ex-div status.

✓ In this case P_a = today's share price – present value of the next dividend.

4 SENSITIVITY OF OPTION PRICES

4.1 Delta

✓ Delta measures the sensitivity of an option's price to a change in the market price of the underlying asset.

✓ Delta of a call = $N(d_1)$

✓ Delta of a put = $N(d_1) - 1$

4.2 Delta Hedging

✓ Delta is also referred to as "the hedge ratio" and can be used to construct a risk-free portfolio containing an underlying asset and options on that asset.

✓ The number of options required in the hedge is dictated by delta – ensuring that any losses on the underlying asset are perfectly offset by gains on the options.

4.3 Gamma

✗ Delta itself is not a constant and is only accurate for very small changes in the price of the underlying asset.

✓ Gamma measures the sensitivity of delta to changes in the price of the underlying asset.

4.4 Theta

- ✓ Measures the impact of time decay on the value of an option.

4.5 Vega

- ✓ Measures the impact of a change in the volatility of the underlying asset on the value of an option.

4.6 Rho

- ✓ Measures the impact of a change in interest rates on the value of an option.

5 REAL OPTIONS PRICING THEORY (ROPT)

5.1 Approach

- ✓ Traditional NPV fails to capture the value of strategic options that may be "embedded" within a company project.
- ✓ These are known as "real options" as they are options within physical projects, as opposed to being derivatives.
- ✓ True NPV = traditional NPV + value of embedded options.

5.2 Real Option Archetypes

(1) A delay or "wait and see" option (e.g. an option to buy (*call*) a piece of land for a potential construction project).

(2) An abandonment or "exit" option – having the right to sell (*put*) the project to a third party.

(3) An expansion option – for example based on the initial success of the "iPod" Apple Inc was able to launch (*call*) further projects (the "iPhone" and then the "iPad" and then the "iWatch").

(4) A redeployment or "flexibility" option (e.g. investing in Flexible Manufacturing Systems (FMS) that, if necessary, the firm can *call* to perform alternative functions).

5.3 Critique of ROPT

- ✓ Investors may be aware of which firms have the flexibility of real options and be prepared to pay more for the shares and bonds of such firms, lowering the WACC and increasing the NPV of potential projects.
- ✗ Therefore traditional NPV may already reflect the value of real options in which case adding their value is double-counting.

5.4 Applying ROPT to Value Intangible Assets

✓ Holding a patent on a potential product has the characteristics of a "delay" option and can be valued using Black-Scholes.

✗ However complications arise as although there is value in being to "wait and see" what happens to market conductions, the longer the firm waits the less the remaining life of the patent.

6 MERTON'S MODELS

6.1 Valuing Equity as an Option

✓ Merton applies the Black-Scholes model to value a firm's equity.

✓ Shareholders can be viewed as conceptually holding a *call* option over the firm's assets, the exercise price being amount required to pay off the firm's debt on maturity.

6.2 Merton's Structural Debt Model

✓ Having found the fair value of equity the following steps can be taken:

1. Fair value of assets – fair value of equity = fair value of debt.

2. By comparing the fair value of debt to its face value, the required yield can be implied.

3. Yield – risk free rate = credit spread.

✓ Furthermore $N(d_2)$ measures the probability that the value of the firm's assets will exceed the amount required to pay off the firm's debt on maturity.

✓ Therefore $N(d_2)$ -1 measures the probability that the firm will default.

1 FORECASTING EXCHANGE RATES

1.1 Relevance

- Firms involved in importing and/or exporting are clearly exposed to potential changes in exchange rates.
- However even firms which buy and sell locally may have to compete with overseas suppliers.

1.2 Purchasing Power Parity (PPP)

- PPP states that exchange rates will change due to different inflation rates in different countries.

Published formula

- $S_1 = S_0 \times \dfrac{(1 + h_c)}{(1 + h_b)}$

Where:

S_1 = the forecast spot exchange rate
S_0 = today's spot exchange rate
h_b = the domestic inflation rate
h_c = the overseas inflation rate

1.3 Interest Rate Parity (IRP)

- IRP claims that the forward exchange rate reflects the difference in interest rates between two countries.

Published formula

- $F_0 = S_0 \times \dfrac{(1 + i_c)}{(1 + i_b)}$

Where:

F_0 = the forward exchange rate
i_b = the domestic interest rate
i_c = the overseas interest rate

1.4 Expectations Theory

- Forward exchange rates are expected spot rates.

1.5 Balance of Trade

- If a country has a trade deficit (where imports exceed exports) then the supply of its currency on the foreign exchange market will exceed the demand.
- The value of the currency will therefore fall – making imports more expensive and exports more competitive.
- Imports fall and exports rise – leading to a potential elimination of the trade deficit.

2 TYPES OF EXCHANGE RATE RISK

2.1 Translation Risk

✓ Assets and liabilities of overseas subsidiaries must be translated into the reporting currency of the parent prior to consolidation into the group financial statements.

✓ This creates potentially large currency translation gains/losses – however these are simply caused by accounting rules and do not reflect cash gains/losses.

2.2 Economic Risk

✗ The risk that cash flows will be affected by *long-term* exchange rate movements.

✗ For example an exporter's cash flows will be damaged if its home currency tends to appreciate over time.

✗ This is a real risk but cannot be effectively hedged using financial instruments as the price of currency in the derivatives markets follows the same long-term trend as in the spot market.

2.3 Transaction Risk

✗ The risk that the exchange rate changes between the date of a specific export/import and the related receipt/payment of foreign currency.

✓ This is a real risk which *can* be effectively hedged using derivatives.

2.4 Internal Management of Exchange Rate Risk

✓ Invoice in domestic currency.

✓ Leading and lagging – pay overseas suppliers quickly if the home currency is expected to fall, and slowly if expected to rise.

✓ Netting – net foreign currency receivables and payables before considering an external hedge on the balance.

✓ Matching – finance overseas subsidiaries with foreign currency debt.

3 EXTERNAL HEDGING STRATEGIES

3.1 Forward Exchange Contracts

With Physical Delivery

- ✓ A forward contract is a legally binding agreement between a company and a bank to buy/sell a fixed amount of foreign exchange on a fixed date at a fixed rate.

- ✓ Provides the company with a short-term fixed exchange rate which protects against downside risk.

- ✗ No upside potential as the forward contract is legally binding and must be exercised even if its gives a worse outcome than the future spot rate.

Non-deliverable Forwards (NDFs)

- ✓ A "contract for differences" – on settlement date the contracted rate is benchmarked against spot and compensation paid/received based on the difference.

3.2 Money Market Hedges

- ✓ An exporter could borrow foreign currency, convert it into local currency and later use the export earnings to repay the foreign currency loan.

- ✓ In this way the company has generated a fixed amount of local currency from its export earnings – it has produced a short-term fixed exchange rate which theoretically should equal the forward rate.

- ✓ An *importer* would initially deposit foreign currency and later use this deposit plus the interest received to pay their overseas supplier.

3.3 Currency Options

Terminology

- ✓ The holder of an option has the right, but not the obligation, to buy (if *calls*) or sell (if *puts*) a fixed amount of a stated currency at a fixed price (the *exercise price*) on or before a fixed date (the *expiry date*).

- ✓ The holder of an option can later choose whether or not to exercise it – hence options can protect against downside risk while allowing upside potential.

- ✗ This flexibility comes at a cost – a "premium" must be paid to acquire the option.

FOREIGN EXCHANGE RISK MANAGEMENT

Hedging With Options

1. Should options be purchased (held) or sold (written)? For risk management the default approach is to *purchase* options and hence *pay* a premium (to the writer).

2. Puts or calls? This depends on the specific situation. For example, a firm exporting to euroland wanting the *right to sell* its export earnings should purchase *puts* on the euro.

3. Expiry date? Use an expiry date that at least covers the period of underlying risk.

4. Strike price? *Choose* a strike price and justify the choice, for example the closest strike price to spot sets up the hedge "near the money".

5. How many options? Compare the size of the underlying exposure to the size of each option.

6. What is the total premium to be paid? Note the premium is paid in advance.

7. Expected outcome of the hedge? Demonstrate this under the assumption that the options will be exercised.

Delta Hedging With Currency Options

✓ Delta is the change in an option's price for a (small) change in the price of the underlying asset (in this case the spot exchange rate).

✓ Knowledge of delta can be used to construct a "delta hedge" where gains/losses on an options position perfectly offset losses/gains on an underlying exposure.

✗ Unfortunately delta is not a constant and hence the hedge has to be frequently rebalanced, creating high transaction costs.

3.4 Currency Futures Contracts

The Nature of Futures

✓ The definition of a futures contract is the same as for a forward contract.

✓ However hedging with futures is very different because "physical delivery" does not occur on the futures market.

✗ This means the firm cannot actually buy or sell foreign exchange using futures contracts.

✓ However if a futures hedge is correctly performed a gain on the futures market will offset a loss made on the spot currency market (and vice versa).

Hedging With Futures

1. Should the firm initially buy or sell futures ("long" or "short" position)? This depends on the specific situation. For example, a firm exporting to euroland needing protection again a falling euro should *sell* euro futures – a short position makes a gain on a falling price.
2. Which expiry date? Use a contract with an expiry date that at least covers the period of underlying risk.
3. How many contracts? Compare the size of the underlying exposure to the size of each contract.
4. Expected outcome of the hedge? Whether the spot rate rises or falls the overall outcome for the firm should be the same as a futures hedge, like a forward hedge, produces an (approximately) fixed result.

The Tick System

✓ Tick size = the minimum price change recognised by the futures market.

✓ Tick value = the monetary gain/loss on one futures contract for a one tick price change.

The Margining System

✓ Initial margin = a security deposit that all participants on the futures market must "post" in their brokerage account to prevent default.

✓ Maintenance margin = the level to which margin can fall (if losses are incurred) before the market makes "margin call" for replenishment.

Marking to Market

✓ At the end of each trading day each participant's futures contracts are "marked to market" and gains/losses accrued.

Comparison of Futures With Forward Contracts

✓ Futures are standardised, forwards can be customised.

✓ Futures are exchange traded, forwards are OTC.

✓ Futures have no default risk, forwards have (small) default risk.

✓ Futures are settled by offset (reversing the buy/sell decision to close the hedge), forwards are (usually) settled by physical delivery.

✓ A futures hedge gives an *approximately* fixed outcome (futures prices may not behave as expected – *basis risk*) whereas a forward contract gives a certain outcome.

3.5 Currency Swaps

To reduce the cost of foreign currency debt

✓ Suppose a UK company wishes to borrow $. Although the company is well known in the UK and can obtain £ at competitive interest rates it does not have an established relationship with US banks and is not offered attractive $ interest rates.

✓ However if it can find a US company that can borrow $ cheaply but actually wants £ then a currency swap could be arranged to benefit both parties. It would operate as follows:

(1) The UK company borrows £, the US company borrows $ i.e. each company borrows in the market where it has a comparative advantage.

(2) There is an initial exchange of principals at an agreed exchange rate, usually spot rate.

(3) Over the life of the swap there will be an exchange of interest payments i.e. the UK company will pay $ interest to the US company and will receive £ interest from the US company.

(4) At the end of the swap there is a re-exchange of principals at an agreed exchange rate (usually the original) spot rate.

For hedging

✓ A "plain vanilla" currency swap is a series of forward exchange rates written into an OTC contract between two counterparties (e.g. a bank and its client).

✓ Currency swaps can potentially be agreed for several years and therefore hedge currency economic risk.

Valuation of Plain Vanilla Currency Swaps

✓ The fixed exchange rate in a currency swap should be the weighted average of the forward exchange rates for the relevant period.

FX Swaps

✓ An exchange of principals at prevailing spot, *no* annual exchange of cash flows, then a re-exchange of principals at the end of the swap (at a pre-agreed rate).

1 NATURE OF INTEREST RATE RISK

1.1 Exposure to Rising Interest Rates

- A firm with variable "floating" interest rate debt will pay more interest if rates rise.

1.2 Exposure to Falling Interest Rates

- A firm with investments producing variable interest rate income will see its profits fall if rates fall.

1.3 Other Types of Interest Rate Risk

- Basis risk – even if a firm has both floating rate assets and floating rate liabilities they may be linked to different benchmark interest rates which may move by different amounts.

- Gap exposure:
    - negative gap – floating rate liabilities > floating rate assets;
    - positive gap – floating rate assets > floating rate liabilities.

1.4 Internal Management of Interest Rate Risk

- Smoothing – having a balance between floating and fixed-rate debt.

- Matching floating rate debt to floating rate assets and fixed rate debt to fixed rate assets,

- Asset and liability management – matching assets and liabilities not only to the same interest rate but also to the same maturity date.

2 EXTERNAL HEDGING STRATEGIES

2.1 Forward Rate Agreements

- FRAs allow companies to fix, in advance, either a future borrowing rate or a future deposit rate.

- An FRA is a "contract for differences" – on settlement date the contracted rate is benchmarked against prevailing LIBOR (London Inter Bank Offered Rate).

- Compensation is then paid/received based on the difference and the agreed face value of the FRA.

2.2 OTC Options

- Cap – protects debts against rising rates but allows participation in falling rates.

- Floor – protects investment income against falling yields but allows participation in rising yields.

- Collar – a combination of a cap and floor – creates an interest rate band.

INTEREST RATE RISK MANAGEMENT

2.3 Interest Rate Futures

Characteristics of IRFs

✓ IRFs represent *notional* loans – a firm cannot actually borrow or invest money using IRFs as there is no physical delivery.

✓ Market price is based on (zero-coupon) treasury bills (which always trade at a discount to face value).

✓ Market price of IRF = 100 – implied interest rate.

Hedging With IRFs

1. Should the firm initially buy or sell futures ("long" or "short" position)? This depends on the specific situation. For example, a firm wanting protection against rising interest rates should take a *short* position (as rising interest rates lead to *falling* prices of IRFs).

2. Which expiry date? Use a contract with an expiry date that at least covers the period of underlying risk.

3. How many contracts ? Compare:

   ➢ the *principal* of the physical loan to the face value of the IRF; **and**

   ➢ the *duration* of the physical loan to the notional duration of the loan beneath the IRF.

4. Expected outcome of the hedge? Whether LIBOR rises or falls the overall outcome for the firm should be the same as a futures hedge, like a forward hedge, produces an (approximately) fixed result.

2.4 Options on Futures Contracts

✓ To hedge against rising interest rates, but also benefit if rates fall, the firm would like the right, but not the obligation, to sell IRFs.

✓ Therefore *buy puts* to create an interest rate *cap*.

✓ To hedge against falling yields on investments, but also benefit if rates rise, the firm would like the right, but not the obligation, to buy IRFs.

✓ Therefore *buy calls* to create an interest rate *floor*.

✓ To hedge against rising interest rates, but also benefit to some degree if rates fall – *buy puts* and *sell calls* to create a *low-cost cap* (collar).

✓ To hedge against falling yields on investments, but also benefit to some degree if rates rise – *buy calls* and *sell puts* to create a *low-cost floor* (collar).

2.5 Interest Rate Swaps

Nature and uses

- ✓ A "plain vanilla" interest rate swap is an exchange of a floating interest rate (LIBOR) for a fixed interest rate.

- ✓ Swap is settled annually in arrears – based on the difference between LIBOR and the fixed rate in the swap, multiplied by the agreed face value of the swap.

- ✓ The main uses of interest rate swaps are:
  - ➢ to reduce the firm's cost of debt; and
  - ➢ to hedge interest rate risk.

Exploiting comparative advantage

- ✓ A swap may be arranged, via a bank, between two companies.

- ✓ If one company has a comparative strength in fixed rates (perhaps due to a good reputation with the bond market) but actually desires a floating rate it should:
  - ➢ issue fixed rate bonds;
  - ➢ use the swap to transform its position to a floating rate (which could be lower than it would achieve through direct borrowing in floating rate markets).

- ✓ The counterparty would issue floating rate debt and use the swap to indirectly move into a fixed rate (perhaps to hedge against rising rates).

Swap between a bank and its client

- ✓ Sometimes banks will themselves enter into swaps with their clients.

- ✓ When a bank sets the fixed rate in a swap it should be equivalent, in present value terms, to the expected floating rate payments.

- ✓ The bank does not know what LIBOR will be in future but can look at "forward interest rates" for guidance.

- ✓ Forward interest rates are rates that relate to borrowing money between two dates in the future (e.g. FRA rates).

Swaptions

- ✓ Swaption – a "hybrid" derivative combining the flexibility of an option with the potential benefits of a swap.

1 MULTINATIONAL CORPORATIONS

1.1 Background

✓ The rise of the multinational appears to be unstoppable, particularly with the continuing consolidation in many sectors via M&As.

1.2 Competitive Advantage

✓ Multinationals enjoy advantages such as:

> economies of scale;
> natural internal currency hedges;
> opportunities for reducing tax via transfer pricing;
> political power.

2 INTERNATIONAL TRADE

2.1 International Trade v Protectionism

✓ There is a global trend for the removal of trade barriers, with increasing number of countries joining the World Trade Organisation (WTO), etc.

✗ However certain countries have become increasingly protectionist, particularly following the global financial crisis of 2008.

✗ Furthermore, whilst "free trade areas" promote liberalisation within their borders they tend to be protectionist towards non-members.

2.2 Free Trade Areas

✓ European Union – formed in 1993 as a single market for goods, services, labour and capital. Currently has 28 member countries.

✓ North American Free Trade Area (NAFTA) –formed in 1993 as a free trade area between the USA, Canada and Mexico.

✓ Association of South East Asian States (ASEAN) – formed in 1967 and comprises the Philippines, Malaysia, Thailand, .Indonesia, Singapore and Vietnam.

✓ WTO – formed in 1995 and currently has 161 member countries. Its goal is "to help producers of goods and services, exporters, and importers conduct their business."

2.3 Mobility of Capital

- ✓ In recent decades many barriers to the international movement of capital have been removed.
- ✓ The banking and financial services sectors are now very much global in nature due the falling incidence of exchange controls and technological advances.
- ✗ However some countries, particularly developing nations, still impose capital controls such as:
  - ➢ blocks on foreign direct investment (FDI) into strategically sensitive sectors (e.g. defence or banking);
  - ➢ limits on convertibility of currency;
  - ➢ blocks on payment of dividends to overseas parents.
- ✓ A multinational corporation needs an approach to mitigate the impact of such capital controls, for example:
  - ➢ joint ventures with overseas partners;
  - ➢ political lobbying to ensure convertibility;
  - ➢ financing overseas investments with loans from the parent.

3 INTERNATIONAL FINANCE

3.1 Exchange-Rate Systems

Floating Exchange Rates

- ✓ No central bank intervention in the currency market and hence the exchange rate rises/falls without limits.

Fixed Peg

- ✓ Where the value of the domestic currency is fixed against a foreign currency or "basket" of foreign currencies.

Crawling Peg

- ✓ Where the exchange rate is allowed to rise/fall within a narrow band around a "peg". The peg can be periodically reset if required.

3.2 International Financial Institutions

- ✓ In 1944 the Bretton Woods Conference established the International Bank for Reconstruction and Development (now part of the World Bank) and the International Monetary Fund (IMF).

- ✓ World Bank – is a vital source of financial and technical assistance to developing countries. Provides low-interest loans and grants to support areas such as education, health, agriculture, and environmental and natural resource management.

- ✓ IMF – an organisation of 188 countries working towards global monetary cooperation, financial stability, free international trade and sustainable economic growth around the world.

3.3 Role of Central Banks

- ✓ US Federal Reserve ("the Fed") – has a mandate to "promote sustainable growth, high levels of employment, stability of prices to help preserve the purchasing power of the dollar and moderate long-term interest rates".

- ✓ Bank of England (BoE) – exists to secure the UK's monetary stability and enhance the stability of the financial system.

- ✓ European Central Bank (ECB) – manages the euro but works closely with *all* 28 members of the EU, even those (e.g. the UK) which are outside of the Eurozone.

- ✓ Bank of Japan (BoJ) – main objectives are price stability and financial stability.

3.4 Global Debt

- ✓ The 2005 G8 summit wrote off $40 billion owed by developing nations to the World Bank, IMF and African Development Bank.

- ✗ However the G8 countries themselves (and many other developed nations) had enormous amounts of public and private debt – ultimately leading to the global financial crisis of 2008 which for countries such as Greece still continues.

3.5 Islamic Finance

Principles

- ✓ Profits should only be made from socially acceptable value- added business activities.

- ✓ Prohibited activities include the payment or receipt of interest, excessive use of debt, investing in immoral activities, speculation and complex derivatives.

Islamic Business Structures

- ✗ Islam does not recognise the concept of a company being a spate legal entity from its owners.

- ✓ Therefore partnership is the preferred business structure.

Islamic Banks

✓ Islamic banks offer both equity-based and fixed-income based products.

Equity-Based Financial Products

✓ Mudaraba – pure equity finance.

✓ Musharaka – joint venture or partnership.

Fixed-Income-Based Financial Products

✓ Murabaha – trade credit

✓ Ijara – leasing

✓ Salam – where a commodity is sold today (at a discount) for immediate payment but delivery occurs on a future date.

✓ Sukuk bonds – certificates of equal value representing ownership of the tangible assets of a particular project.

Sharia Boards

✓ Ensures that all products offered by Islamic financial institutions do comply with the principles of Sharia law.

Benefits of Islamic Finance

✓ Clarity regarding the subject matter and terms of a contract (in contrast to the intangible and complex nature of derivatives).

✓ Debt should be serviced by specific physical projects and not used excessively.

✓ Investors in partnerships and joint ventures scrutinise proposed projects with great care, thereby promoting a stable economy.

✓ Vetting of financial products by the Sharia board provides independent oversight.

Drawbacks

✗ Agency problems in Musharaka contracts – potential conflict between the bank and the entrepreneur.

✗ Islamic scholars have different interpretations of Sharia law – an instrument deemed compliant in one country may be deemed non-compliant in another.

✗ Slow approval process by Sharia boards can limit innovation.

3.6 Sukuk Finance

Asset-Based Sukuk

✓ The principal is covered by the capital value of the asset but the repayments are not directly financed by these assets.

Asset-Backed Sukuk

✓ The principal is covered by the capital value of the asset but the repayments *are directly* financed by these assets.

Recent developments

✓ In 2014 the UK became the first country outside the Islamic world to issue a sovereign "sukuk" bond.

✓ The UK sukuk bond is serviced from the rental income on specific properties owned by the government.

4 EMERGING ISSUES

4.1 Securitisation and the Global Financial Crisis

✓ Securitisation is the pooling and selling of illiquid assets as tradable instruments known generally as Asset Backed Securities (ABS).

✓ The classic example is Mortgage Backed Securities (MBS) where banks sell blocks of home loans to raise cash to lend again (often to property speculators) in an endless cycle of credit creation.

✓ A portfolio of MBS can even be "chopped up" into different "tranches" of risk as in the case of Collateralised Debt Obligations (CDOs) – a complex derivative instrument common in the sub-prime mortgage market.

✗ Many blame the securitisation process for inflating asset prices (e.g. the property price bubble that preceded the 2008 global financial crisis).

✗ When the bubble burst there was a "death spiral" as the when the value of CDOs stated to fall, financial institutions holding them had to write down them down under "mark to market" accounting rules.

- ✗ One an institutions' fair value of assets fell towards its level of liabilities it was forced to liquidate the holdings, causing the price of CDOs to fall further.

4.2 Dark Pools

- ✓ These are share dealing networks created by investment banks to allow their clients to execute trades away from the public stock markets.

- ✓ Dark pool trading is particularly popular with hedge funds that use secretive algorithm- based trading strategies and do not wish their trades to be known to the public.

- ✗ Critics of dark pools view them as "opaque" and unfair to other investors.

- ✓ Supporters if dark pools state that they encourage active trading and increase market efficiency.

4.3 Financial Contagion

- ✓ Financial contagion refers to the increasing interdependence of world markets due to "globalisation". The effects of this can clearly be seen as global equity markets often appear to follow New York's lead.

- ✗ This has led to increasing correlation coefficients between markets, reducing the risk reduction benefits of global diversification.

- ✓ Some countries initially believed they were sufficiently "decoupled" from the American economy to be isolated from the 2008 sub-prime crisis.

- ✗ Regrettably in the end it does appear that "when the USA sneezes, the rest of the world catches a cold".

4.4 Developments in Derivatives

- ✓ A credit default swap is an insurance policy against default on an underlying bond. A gigantic notional principal of CDSs had been written against default on sub-prime mortgage backed securities.

- ✗ Many argue that the growth in the market for credit default swaps (CDSs) was one of the contributory factors to the global financial crisis.

- ✗ Risk can be packaged (into MBS), repackaged (into CDO) and transferred (using CDS) but risk does not evaporate – sadly it takes a financial crises to reveal it.

- ✓ Credit default swaps are part of the OTC derivatives market - they are traded face to face as opposed to via an exchange.

*   This creates a problem for regulators as the OTC market is opaque. Many governments, particularly the American government, therefore want to move the OTC markets onto formal exchanges.

*   Some even advocate a unified global exchange for all derivatives although this could bring its own dangers – what would happen of this global exchange collapsed?

4.5 Special Purpose Vehicles (SPVs)

✓   SPVs can be legitimately used to achieve an enhanced credit rating by diverting relatively high quality cash flows (e.g. rental income) into the SPV which is ring-fenced should the parent become distressed.

✓   The SPV (often established offshore) then uses its enhanced credit rating to issue asset backed securities (ABS) at a low interest rate.

*   Unfortunately SPVs have also been abused, most famously by Enron which used hundreds of such entities (which were not consolidated into its group accounts) to hide its liabilities.

4.6 Increasing Transparency of Tax Havens

✓   The OECD (Organisation for Economic Cooperation and Development) is putting increasing pressure on tax havens to become more transparent.

✓   The US authorities are particularly unhappy about the use of the Cayman Islands for both tax avoidance and the hiding of "toxic assets".

✓   International anti-money laundering laws are also pressurising offshore regimes to increase their disclosure requirements.

✓   Note that US parent companies are only taxed on overseas profits that are remitted back to the US – hence many keep the cash offshore.

✓   This explains why in 2013 Apple Inc. had to make a record bond issue ($17 billion) to finance its share buyback programme – despite generating huge cash flows from its global operations Apple Inc. is not inclined to remit the cash back to the US where it would be taxed at 35%.

1 INTERNATIONAL TRADE RISKS

1.1 Foreign Exchange Risks

- Exporting will expose the firm to both short-term transaction risk and long-term economic risk.

1.2 Credit Risk

- A key risk when exporting is of bad debts.
- This can be reduced by requesting a letter of credit from the overseas customer's bank.

1.3 Physical Risk

- Goods may be lost or damaged in transit – appropriate insurance will cover this.

1.4 Political Risk

- Quotas, tariffs, currency controls, slow customs clearance – such problems can at least be evaluated in advance with appropriate research (e.g. using the Economist Intelligence Unit www.eiu.com).

1.5 Cultural Risk

- Lack of knowledge of local business practices and etiquette.
- Overseas embassies and trade missions may advise.

1.6 Payment Methods

- Open account trading – simply trusting the overseas customer to pay.
- Cash against documents – not releasing legal title to the goods until payment is received.
- Bill of exchange – a document signed by the overseas customer promising to pay a fixed sum on a fixed date. The bill can either be held to maturity or immediately sold (at a discount) to a bank.
- Forfaiting – selling a series of bills to a bank at a discount.
- Use an export merchant – the firm sells to the merchant (for immediate payment) who then resells to the overseas customer.
- Counter-Trade – receiving payments in a commodity rather than cash, potentially due to currency controls.

2 OVERSEAS EXPANSION

2.1 Methods

- ✓ Exporting
- ✓ Licensing
- ✓ Joint venture
- ✓ Overseas subsidiary

2.2 Political Risk

- ✗ Highest in the case of an overseas subsidiary with the potential for appropriation of assets.
- ✓ Mitigation techniques include using local finance for those assets.

3 INTERNATIONAL TREASURY FUNCTION

3.1 Role of International Treasury

- ✓ Treasury involves the efficient management of liquidity and risk including the management of interest rates, currencies and cash flow.
- ✓ In an international context tax planning regarding dividend remittances and transfer pricing also becomes relevant.

3.2 Cost Centre v Profit Centre

- ✓ It may be advisable to classify the treasury department as a cost centre as classification as a profit centre could lead to risk-taking and speculation.

3.3 Centralised v Decentralised

Advantages of Centralised Treasury Management

- ✓ Economies of scale (e.g. combining group borrowing requirements).
- ✓ "Pooling" of cash surpluses and deficits.
- ✓ Multilateral netting – minimising the number of transactions between group companies by finding the net amounts to be paid in terms of a common currency.
- ✓ Identifying natural internal hedges on currencies and interest rates.
- ✓ Optimising transfer prices and dividend remittances for tax purposes.
- ✓ Specialised knowledge of global finance such the use of Special Purposes Vehicles (SPVs) for credit enhancement.

Disadvantages of Centralised Treasury Management

- ✗ Agency issues – potential conflict between head office and overseas subsidiaries.
- ✗ Head office may lack understanding of the overseas laws, regulations and business culture.

4 INTERNATIONAL CAPITAL BUDGETING

4.1 Net Present Value

(1) Forecast the overseas cash flows expressed in foreign currency.

(2) Forecast the exchange rate that will apply at the time of each cash flow, using Purchasing Power Parity if forecast inflation rates are given or Interest Rate Parity if interest rates are given.

(3) Convert all cash flows into the home currency and add any cash flows arising in the home country (e.g. additional tax on overseas earnings).

(4) Find the appropriate WACC – reflecting the specific business risk of the project (note that political risk is an element of business risk).

(5) Discount to find NPV in home currency terms.

4.2 Adjusted Present Value (APV)

- ✓ If the overseas project's finance will disturb the firm's existing capital structure then APV may be appropriate.
- ✓ The "base-case NPV" would be founds using the steps shown above (except the ungeared cost of equity should be used as the discount rate).
- ✓ Present value of tax shield and any side-effects are found by discounting the related cash flows in (in *home currency* terms) at the *home country* pre-tax cost of debt.

5 INTERNATIONAL CAPITAL STRUCTURE

- ✓ If an overseas subsidiary is to be established then the capital structure decision needs to take into account the opportunity to hedge currency risk and political risk.
- ✓ Issuing part of the equity, and potentially all debt, to local investors may mitigate the risk of aggressive tactics by the host government.
- ✓ If debt is to be raised then denominating it in the foreign currency proves an effective long-term hedge against currency economic risk.

6 TRANSFER PRICING

6.1 Global Tax Planning

✓ Multinational corporations have an opportunity to use transfer pricing to shift profits from high tax jurisdictions to low tax jurisdictions, as well as minimising import duties on the transfer of physical goods between group companies.

✓ The greatest opportunity may be for technology firms who can make recharges for items such as the use of intellectual capital.

✓ A famous example is Google's use of the "double Irish with a Dutch sandwich" – an Irish subsidiary transfers profits to a Dutch subsidiary which then transfers them back to another Irish subsidiary which is not tax resident in Ireland as its headquarters are located in the Cayman Islands.

✓ Furthermore provided that Google's overseas profits are not remitted back to the US they are exempt from 35% US corporate tax.

✓ Note that from 1 January 2015 the "double Irish" loophole has been closed as any company registered in the Republic of Ireland will be classed as tax resident.

6.2 Impact on Reputational and Regulatory Risk

✓ In 2014 the European Commission launched an investigation into Apple Inc.'s use of a variant on the "Double Irish".

✓ Starbucks Inc. is also under investigation regards its low-tax Dutch subsidiary which appears to record much of its profits from across Europe.

✓ Aggressive tax avoidance schemes are increasingly being challenged both by regulators and consumers.

✓ A company which wishes to mitigate such risks may consider following the OECD's transfer pricing guidelines and apply for the "Fair Tax Mark".

✓ http://www.fairtaxmark.net/

1 ANALYSIS OF FINANCIAL STATEMENTS

- ✓ The senior financial executive needs to be aware of how their financing and investing decision may impact on the ratios used by investors and their advisors.

2 PERFORMANCE RATIOS

- ✓ Return on capital employed (ROCE) =
$$\frac{\text{Profit before interest and tax}}{\text{Shareholders' funds + non - current liabilities}} \times 100$$

- ✓ Return on equity (ROE) =
$$\frac{\text{Profit after tax - preference dividends}}{\text{Ordinary shareholders' funds}} \times 100$$

- ✓ Gross profit margin = $\frac{\text{Gross profit}}{\text{Sales}} \times 100$

- ✓ Operating margin = $\frac{\text{EBIT}}{\text{Sales}} \times 100$

3 LIQUIDITY RATIOS

Current ratio = $\frac{\text{Current assets}}{\text{Current liabilities}}$

Quick or acid test ratio = $\frac{\text{Current assets - inventory}}{\text{Current liabilities}}$

Debt to equity = $\frac{\text{Non - current liabilities}}{\text{Capital + reserves}} \times 100$

Debt to total capital = $\frac{\text{Non - current liabilities}}{\text{Capital employed}} \times 100$

Interest Cover =
$$\frac{\text{Profit before interest and tax}}{\text{Interest expense}} \times 100$$

Operational Gearing =

$$\frac{\text{Fixed operating costs}}{\text{Variable operating costs}} \times 100 \text{ or}$$

$$\frac{\text{Fixed operating costs}}{\text{Total operating costs}} \times 100$$

FINANCIAL STATEMENT ANALYSIS

4 EFFICIENCY RATIOS

$$\text{Inventory days} = \frac{\text{Average inventory}}{\text{Annual cost of sales}} \times 365$$

Receivable days =

$$\frac{\text{Average accounts receivable}}{\text{Annual credit sales}} \times 365$$

Payable days =

$$\frac{\text{Average accounts payable}}{\text{Annual credit purchases}} \times 365$$

Cash conversion cycle = inventory days + receivables days – payables days

5 INVESTOR RATIOS

Earnings per ordinary share (EPS) =

$$= \frac{\text{Profit after tax - preference dividends}}{\text{Number of ordinary shares in issue}}$$

Dividend cover = =

$$= \frac{\text{Profit after tax - preference dividend}}{\text{Ordinary dividend}}$$

Dividend payout ratio =

$$\frac{\text{Ordinary dividend}}{\text{Profit after tax - preference dividend}}$$

Dividend yield =

$$\frac{\text{Dividend per ordinary share}}{\text{Ordinary share price}} \times 100$$

Price/earnings ratio (P/E ratio) =

$$\frac{\text{Ordinary share price}}{\text{EPS}}$$

$$\text{Earnings yield} = \frac{\text{EPS}}{\text{Ordinary share price}} \times 100$$

Total Shareholder Return (TSR) =

$$\frac{\text{Year - end share price + dividends}}{\text{Share price at start of year}} \times 100$$

6 ECONOMIC VALUE ADDED

EVA™ = post-tax operating profit – (capital employed × WACC)

ADDITIONAL READING

- *student accountant* – the most useful articles have been summarised in earlier sections of these notes. However be sure to check the ACCA website in the weeks leading up to the exam in case any new articles appear

- Reference texts – Becker's Study System is designed as a comprehensive study text. If you wish for more detail on topics covered in the syllabus the following texts are recommended:

    Arnold, G., Corporate Financial Management

    Damodaran, A., Investment Valuation: Tools and Techniques for Determining the Value of Any Asset

    http://pages.stern.nyu.edu/~adamodar

    Hull, J., Fundamentals of Futures and Options Markets,

- Additional marks can be awarded to candidates who give relevant real-life examples to support their discussion. Reading quality financial press is therefore useful, for example:

    The Financial Times www.ft.com

    The Economist www.economist.com

    CFO www.cfo.com

SECURITISATION AND TRANCHING

This section is based on an article by a member of the P4 examining team. The article appeared in "student accountant" and can be found at http://www.accaglobal.co.uk/en/student/acca-qual-student-journey/qual-resource/acca-qualification/p4/technical-articles.html

Introduction

Securitisation refers to the process of converting an illiquid asset into cash.

An early example was the "Bowie bond" issued in 1997 – a US$55m 10-year A-rated bond paying 7.9% (10-year Treasury notes were paying 6.37% at the time). Interest on the bond was serviced by the future stream of royalties from musician David Bowie's existing catalogue of 25 albums.

The Bowie bond is part of an asset class known as ABS (asset-backed securities). The most notorious segment of the asset class is the MBS (mortgage-backed security) – blamed by many as one of the causes of the global financial crisis of 2007-8.

A particularly complex type of MBS is the collateralised debt obligation (CDO) and the focus of this article is to explain how such instruments operate.

Securitisation of mortgages

When banks provide their customers with mortgages these loans are an asset on the bank's statement of financial position, representing cash flow to the bank in future years through interest payments and eventual repayment of the principal.

By "securitising" these loans the bank:

- ✓ transfers the default risk; and
- ✓ converts the loans back into immediate cash which it can lend again (potentially fuelling a property price bubble).

Securitisation is achieved by transferring the loans to a specifically created company called a "special purpose vehicle" (SPV). The SPV is ring-fenced or "bankruptcy remote" in that its assets cannot be seized even if the bank itself becomes insolvent – the SPV therefore achieves a high credit rating.

In the case of conventional mortgages, the SPV effectively purchases a bank's mortgage book for cash, which is raised through the issue of bonds (MBS) serviced by the future income stream flowing from the mortgage holders.

In the case of sub-prime mortgages, the higher levels of risk require a more complex type of securitisation, achieved by the creation of derivative-style instruments known as CDOs.

The structure of CDOs

Unlike a conventional bond issue, where the risk is spread evenly between all the bond holders, CDOs "chop up" the risk into investment layers or "tranches".

An example of a possible structure for a CDO is as follows. For a pool of mortgages taken over by the SPV, three tranches of CDOs are created:

- ✓ **Tranche 1** (highest risk or "equity" tranche) – normally comprising about 10% of the value of the mortgages in the pool. Throughout the CDOs' life, the equity tranche will absorb any losses due to default by the mortgage holders, up to the point where the principal underpinning the tranche is exhausted (in which case the tranche has become worthless).

- ✓ **Tranche 2** (intermediate risk or "mezzanine" tranche) – also normally represents about 10% of the principal and will absorb any losses not absorbed by the equity tranche until the point at which its principal is also exhausted.

- ✓ **Tranche 3** (AAA or "senior" tranche) consists of the balance of the pool value and will absorb any residual losses.

The proportion of the principal held in each tranche is known as the CDO "structure", and if there is relatively high default risk in the mortgage pool the proportion forming the equity and mezzanine tranches will be relatively high.

When cash flows are received from borrowers in the form of interest payments and loan repayments, these are paid to tranche 3 first until its obligation is fulfilled, then tranche 2, and anything left over is paid to the equity tranche.

These payments represent a cascade or "waterfall" of cash with the investors holding their tranches like buckets. The senior tranches get filled first, the mezzanine holders get filled next and anything left falls into the equity pools at the bottom.

CDOs are, therefore, a mechanism whereby potential losses are transferred to investors with the highest appetite for risk (e.g. hedge funds), leaving the bulk of CDOs' investors (mainly other banks) with a low risk source of cash flow.

CDOs are often "over-collateralised" with the principal in the mortgage pool being greater than the overall face value of the CDO. This is a method of credit enhancement designed to reduce the overall interest rate paid on the CDO.

Example

A bank has made a number of mortgage loans to customers with a total value of $350 million. The mortgages have an average term to maturity of ten years. The net income from the loans is 7% per year.

The bank will use 85% of the mortgage pool as collateral for a securitisation with the following structure:

✓ 75% of the collateral value to support a tranche of A-rated loan notes offering investors 6% per year.

✓ 15% of the collateral value to support a tranche of B-rated loan notes offering investors 11% per year.

✓ 10% of the collateral value to support a tranche of subordinated certificates which are unrated.

Cash inflows

Inflows from mortgages $350m × 7% = $24.5m

Cash outflows

A-rated loan notes

$350m × 85% × 75% × 6% = $13.4m

B-rated loan notes

$350m × 85% × 15% × 11% = $4.9m

Total outflows = $13.4m + $4.9m = $18.3m

Difference in cash flows = $24.5m − $18.3m = $6.2m which is returned to the high-risk unrated certificates.

These certificates have a value of $350m × 85% × 10% = $29.75m.

The return on the certificates is $6.2m/$29.75m = 20.8%. However this return is at risk should there be defaults on the underlying mortgages.

Conclusion

Securitisation of mortgages may be a legitimate way for banks to raise new finance but it can lead to property price bubbles due to the continuous cycle of credit creation.

Furthermore the investors in CDOs must put great faith in the accuracy of the ratings given by the agencies If defaults do occur the investors in the CDO are far removed from the mortgage holder and cannot chase them for payment.

Note that securitisation may also be appropriate for a firm which wants to enhance its credit rating by diverting low-risk cash flows (e.g. rental income from property) into a "ring-fenced" SPV.

This section is based on an article by a member of the P4 examining team. The article appeared in the "student accountant" and can be found at http://www.accaglobal.co.uk/en/student/acca-qual-student-journey/qual-resource/acca-qualification/p4/technical-articles.html

Introduction

In this article, we shall evaluate *project risk* by considering all of the possible outcomes that may arise from a particular business decision, together with their related probabilities of occurring.

Expected values, decision trees and combined probabilities

An *expected value* (EV) summarises all the different possible outcomes by weighting the possible outcomes by their probabilities and then summing the result.

Scenarios where more than one decision has to be taken may require the use of a *decision tree*, with EVs being used to evaluate each of the decisions.

A decision tree is a diagrammatic representation of a situation, where the decision maker needs to consider the logical sequence of events.

A situation of *combined probabilities* arises where an initial event has a particular probability of occurring and the following event, which depends on the first event occurring, has another probability of occurring.

For example if event one has a 0.6 chance of occurring and subsequent event two a 0.75 chance of occurring, then overall the probability of *both* events occurring is:

$0.6 \times 0.75 = 0.45$
i.e. a 45% chance of occurring.

Scenario

Brisport Master Motor Co (Brisport) has recently designed a new component for inclusion into hybrid cars.

The company can either sell the design now for $400,000, or attempt to develop the design into a marketable product. This development would have an initial outlay of $300,000 and the component would take one year to be developed. The component is likely to have a commercial life of five years after development.

The chances of succeeding in developing the design into a marketable product are 80%. If the attempt to develop fails, the design can be sold, in one year's time, for just $200,000.

CONDITIONAL PROBABILITY

If the attempt to develop the design succeeds the company can either sell both the design and the rights to the developed component, or market the component itself.

Selling the design would yield $300,000 in one year's time and $160,000 in royalty payments for each of the five years thereafter (years 2 to 6).

If the component is marketed by Brisport then there is a 75% probability of cash inflows of $440,000 per annum but 25% probability of the component being unpopular, creating cash *outflows* of $55,000 per annum. Both cash flow figures are also for each of years 2 to 6.

Brisport uses a weighted average cost of capital of 7% to discount its future cash flows.

The management of Brisport seeks your advice as to their best course of action.

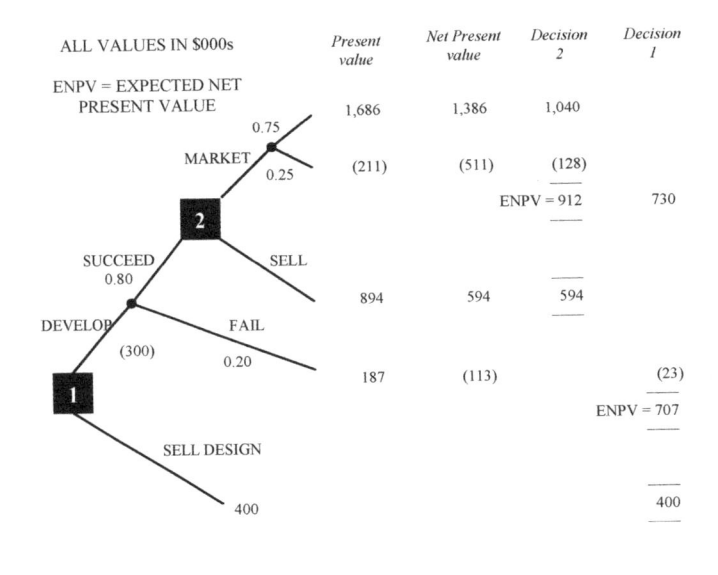

Solution

There are two decisions which need to be made:

1. sell the design immediately or develop it;

2. if it is developed, then whether to sell the design and the production rights, or market the component themselves.

> *Initial workings relating to present value of future cash flows using discount factors at 7% (all values to nearest $000s)*
>
> *Discount factors for T_1 = 0.935*
>
> *Annuity factor ($T_2 - T_6$) 3.832 (Annuity factor ($T_1 - T_6$) − 0.935 = (4.767 − 0.935))*
>
> *"Development fails"*
>
> *Selling the design in one year's time for half of its initial market value: 200 × 0.935 =* **187**
>
> *"Development succeeds"*
>
> *Selling the design in one year's time plus royalties ($T_2 - T_6$) (300 × 0.935) + (160 ×3.832) = 281 + 613 =* **894**
> *Successful marketing of the component ($T_2 - T_6$) 440 ×3.832 =* **1,686**
> *Unsuccessful marketing of the component ($T_2 - T_6$) −55 ×3.832 =* **−211**

In order to evaluate decision 1, decision 2 needs to be evaluated first.

Decision 2

The NPV ($000s) on the 75% path is

1,686 − 300 = 1,386.

Taken together with the NPV ($000s) on the 25% path of

(211) − 300 = (511)

there is an expected NPV of choosing to market the component of ($000s):

[0.75 × 1,386] + [0.25 × (511)]
= 1,040 − 128 = 912

This is a higher value than the option of selling the design and the rights to the developed component for a NPV of $594,000 ($894,000 − $300,000). Therefore, if the development goes ahead, it will be more beneficial to market the product.

We still need to evaluate decision 1, whether to develop at all. The expected present value of $912,000 in decision 2 has an 80% chance of arising, but there is a 20% chance of the development not succeeding and recovering just $187,000 in present value terms, resulting in a loss of $113,000 after taking the development costs into account.

Hence, the expected NPV of the development option of decision 1 can be calculated ($000s):

= [0.80 × 912] + [0.20 × (113)]
= 730 − 23 = 707

Since this is higher than the option to sell the design immediately, the component should be developed and marketed.

Attitude to risk

The EV approach assumes risk neutrality, but not all management decision makers are risk neutral. A risk averse manager would be concerned with the 20% probability of a loss of $113,000 should the development fail.

Furthermore, having taken the decision (at node 2) that marketing the component is preferred to selling both the design and production rights there is a further risk of losses, since there is a 25% chance of the component being unpopular leaving the company worse off by $511,000 in present value terms.

Combined with the 80% probability of the development being successful, there is an overall 80% × 25% = 20% chance of this $511,000 loss. This 20% is known as a *conditional probability* since it depends on the 80% (0.80) success rate firstly and then depends on the 25% (0.25) unpopularity chance.

For completeness, there is of course a 75% chance of the component being popular if marketed, and hence the overall combined probability of a successful development together with a marketing campaign which results in popularity is 80% × 75% = 60%

Summary

Outcome	Probability	NPV ($000s)
Development succeeds and component is popular	60%	1,386
Development succeeds but component is unpopular	20%	(511)
Development fails	20%	(113)

Therefore EVs can lead to a false sense of security. The expected NPV of $707,000 is the average NPV if the decision is repeated over and over again. However this is a one-off development of a product and therefore only one of the outcomes listed in the table above will actually occur.

Furthermore the analysis largely depends on the values of the probabilities prescribed. Often these are subjective estimates made by the decision makers and it would only take relatively small changes in these to alter one of the decisions.

Introduction

The P4 Study Guide contains the following learning outcome "Assess and advise on the impact of investment and financing strategies and decisions on the organisation's stakeholders, from an integrated reporting and governance perspective".

The following section is a précis of "The International Integrated Reporting <IR> Framework" issued by the International, Integrated Reporting Council (IIRC). The full document, and other useful resources, can be found on www.theiirc.org

The IIRC

The IIRC is a global coalition of regulators, investors, companies, standard setters, the accounting profession and NGOs.

The IIRC's vision is a world in which integrated thinking is embedded within mainstream business practice in the public and private sectors, facilitated by Integrated Reporting (<IR>) as the corporate reporting norm.

The cycle of integrated thinking and reporting, resulting in efficient and productive capital allocation, will act as a force for financial stability and sustainability.

Aims of <IR>

- ✓ To improve the quality of information available to providers of financial capital.

- ✓ To communicate the full range of factors that materially affect the ability of an organisation to create value over time.

- ✓ To enhance accountability and stewardship for a broad range of "capitals" and promote understanding of their interdependencies.

- ✓ To support integrated thinking, decision-making and actions that focus on the creation of value over the short, medium and long-term.

"The Capitals"

An integrated report aims to provide insight about the resources and relationships used and affected by an organisation – these are collectively referred to as "the capitals". The capitals are stocks of value that are increased, decreased or transformed through the activities and outputs of the organisation.

Categories

- ✓ Financial capital
- ✓ Manufactured capital
- ✓ Intellectual capital,
- ✓ Human capital
- ✓ Social and relationship capital
- ✓ Natural capital

Guiding Principles

The following principles underpin the preparation of an integrated report:

- ✓ the organisations' strategic focus and future orientation;

- ✓ the factors that affect the organisation's ability to create value over time and the relationships between such factors;

- ✓ the nature and quality of the organisation's relationships with its key stakeholders;

- ✓ materiality;

- ✓ conciseness;

- ✓ reliability and completeness;

- ✓ consistency and comparability.

Content Elements

An integrated report includes eight Content Elements:

1. organisational overview and external environment
2. governance
3. business model
4. risks and opportunities
5. strategy and resource allocation
6. performance – including impacts on "the capitals"
7. outlook
8. basis of presentation

This section is from Paper F9 but is also relevant to Paper P4. For the full article see
http://www.accaglobal.com/gb/en/student/acca-qual-student-journey/qual-resource/acca-qualification/f9/technical-articles.html

Introduction

Managers of large businesses have often been accused of focusing on short-term rather than long-term performance. Managers often prefer projects with a short payback period rather than those with slower, but ultimately higher returns and hence higher NPV.

Such short-sighted or "myopic" behaviour can lead to reduced investment returns, the destruction of shareholder value and a loss in public confidence corporate governance.

Myopic management can be viewed as one element of the "agency problem" i.e. a lack of goal congruence between the objectives of the principal (shareholders) and their agent (management). The resulting loss in potential shareholder wealth can be referred to as "agency costs".

Causes of myopic management

There may be powerful incentives for managers to adopt a short-term focus in order to maximise their own welfare at the expense of shareholder wealth.

These include:

- bonus calculations based on short-term performance;

- promotion prospects linked to short-term performance;

- badly designed performance evaluation systems – for example setting ROCE or ROI as a key performance indicator may discourage managers from making long-term investments as their carrying amount will be high in early years (due to low accumulated depreciation) and reported performance initially low;

- where employee share option plans are close to their maturity date management are incentivised to boost short-run reported results in an attempt to spike up the share price and make a quick personal gain;

- a company policy of rotating managers between divisions will encourage a manager to take a short time horizon whilst at each division, leading to underinvestment in research and development or staff training;

- high management turnover i.e. where managers do not stay with the firm for long periods;

- short executive employment contracts.

* shareholder myopia – shareholders do not possess full information about the firm's long-term cash forecasts and therefore tend to become more focused on short-term profit announcements. In turn management will act to produce results that meet investor expectations.

The evidence for management myopia

A survey of US chief financial officers found that they placed great emphasis on meeting or exceeding two key benchmarks: profits for the same quarter of the previous year and the consensus of analysts' estimates for the current quarter. The survey also found that in order to meet the desired level of quarterly profits nearly 80% would be prepared to cut discretionary spending and more than 55% would be prepared to delay a new investment project.

A more recent survey of executives at UK listed firms found that when given a choice between £250,000 tomorrow and £450,000 in three years' time, the majority chose the former. By doing so, however, they were applying an annual discount rate of more than 20% to the future benefits, which is likely to be much higher than the cost of capital of their business.

Shareholder myopia

As suggested earlier it may be that management myopia is at least partly caused by investor myopia. In the UK, shares of listed businesses are on average held for six months compared with eight years in 1960. As a consequence shareholders are less concerned with the future stream of dividends and more concerned with short-term share price movements which, in turn, are likely to be influenced by short-term profit performance. Furthermore there is less incentive to monitor the behaviour of managers because the benefits of doing so are often long term. The end result is that corporate governance is weakened and managers become less accountable.

Various reasons have been suggested for the rise of short-term investing behaviour:

* quarterly evaluation of investment fund managers' performance;

* speculative activities of hedge funds which engage in "high frequency trading" – strategies carried out automatically by computers to move in and out of share positions in seconds or fractions of a second;

* falling transaction costs due to on-line share dealing allow even small private investors to make gains on short-term share price movements.

Efficient Markets Hypothesis and Behavioural Finance

The fact that some shareholders may adopt a short-term focus is difficult to reconcile with the efficient markets hypothesis (EMH). In an efficient market, the value of a share should reflect the long-term future cash flows arising from holding that share i.e. the share price should equal the present value of the expected future dividend stream.

There is increasing evidence, however, that the stock market is not always efficient and that share prices do deviate from fundamental fair values. The growing body of literature on behavioural finance suggests that shareholders are not always rational when making investment decisions. This can result, among other things, in speculative share price bubbles and extended "bull" runs in share prices.

One recent study examined 624 businesses listed on the UK FTSE and US S&P indices over the period 1980–2009 to see whether the pricing of shares was affected by investor short-termism. According to the study:

"In the UK and US, cash flows five years ahead are discounted at rates more appropriate eight or more years hence; 10-year ahead cash-flows are valued as if 16 or more years ahead; and cash-flows more than 30 years ahead are scarcely valued at all."

Interestingly, there was much greater evidence of investor short termism in the final decade of the study.

Curing myopia

Measures should deal with the incentives that drive the behaviour of both managers and shareholders and the interaction between the two groups. The following are some of the measures that have been proposed:

- ✓ Long-term incentive plans – management rewards should be linked more closely to long-term performance and to the strategic aims of the business. Bonuses should only be paid if performance exceeds benchmarks over several years and share option plans should be set with long maturity periods.

- ✓ Including non-financial indicators in performance evaluation systems – key performance indicators should include areas such as the level of innovation, employee morale and customer satisfaction. The "balanced scorecard" is one attempt at this approach.

- ✓ Long-term employment contracts for management

- ✓ An additional "loyalty dividend" and additional voting rights given to those shareholders who keep their shares for a certain period of time.

MANAGEMENT AND SHAREHOLDER MYOPIA

- ✓ Institutional fund managers should be remunerated with regards to the long-term performance of their investment funds, and their reward structure should be published.

- ✓ A company's annual report should include additional reporting of the long-term prospects of the business – reporting "sustainability" through Triple Bottom Line reporting (financial, environmental and social aspects) is one attempt at this, albeit not mandatory at present.

- ✓ closer interaction between management and shareholders – this has been seen with the rise of "activist investors" but as a minimum shareholders should actually use their voting rights,

- ✓ improved corporate governance – a key element of the UK Combined Code is the role of independent non-executive directors in promoting the interests of shareholders. Employee representatives should also sit on the board.

- ✓ Increased accountability of institutional shareholders – the UK Stewardship Code requires that institutional shareholders disclose how they meet their stewardship responsibilities, how they monitor investee companies, what their voting policies are and so on.

- ✓ Introducing tax on share transfers and increasing capital gains tax on short-term profits from share trading.

INTEREST RATES, BOND AND SWAP VALUATION

This section is based on two articles by the P4 examiner. These articles appeared in "student accountant" and can be found at http://www.accaglobal.co.uk/en/student/acca-qual-student-journey/qual-resource/acca-qualification/p4/technical-articles.html

Introduction

Bonds are often referred to as fixed income securities, to distinguish them from equities, in that they often (but not always) make fixed payments to the bond holders at regular intervals. These fixed interest payments are known as bond coupons. Most corporate bonds are redeemable after a specified period of time. Thus, a "plain vanilla" bond will make regular interest payments and buy back the principal on the redemption date.

Bond valuation

Example 1

How much would an investor pay to purchase a bond today, which is redeemable in four years for its par (face or nominal) value of $100 and which carries an annual coupon of 5% on the par value? The required rate of return (yield to maturity or gross redemption yield) for a bond in this risk class is 4%.

As for any asset valuation, the investor would be willing to pay, at the most, the present value of the future income stream discounted at the required rate of return. Thus, the value of the bond can be determined as follows:

	Year 1	Year 2	Year 3	Year 4
Cash flow	$5	$5	$5	$105
PV	$5 \times 1.04^{-1} =$	$5 \times 1.04^{-2} =$	$5 \times 1.04^{-3} =$	$105 \times 1.04^{-4} =$
	4.81	4.62	4.44	89.75

Value/price (sum of the PV of flows) = $103.62

If the required rate of return (or yield) was 6%, then using the same calculation method, the price of the bond would be $96.53. And where the required rate of return (or yield) is equal to the coupon – 5% in this case – the current price of the bond will be equal to the par value of $100.

Thus, there is an *inverse* relationship between the yield of a bond and its price or value. However, it should be noted that this relationship is not linear, but convex.

Candidates are also expected to be able to deal with:

- ✓ more complicated bonds (e.g. bonds with coupon payments more than once a year and convertible bonds and bonds with warrants attached); and

- ✓ more complicated repayment structures (e.g. mortgage or annuity-type payments).

INTEREST RATES, BOND AND SWAP VALUATION

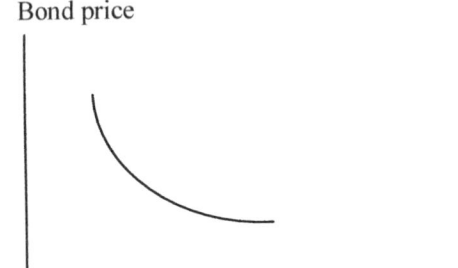

Bond price

Yield (or required return)

Yield to maturity (YTM)/gross redemption yield

If the current price of a bond is given, together with details of coupons and redemption date, then this information can be used to compute the required rate of return or YTM of the bond.

Example 2

A bond paying a coupon of 7% is redeemable in five years at par ($100) and is currently trading at $106.62. The yield can be found as the internal rate of return, r (i.e. the rate that discounts the future cash flows to the market price):

$$106.62 = \$7 \times (1+r)^{-1} + \$7 \times (1+r)^{-2} + \ldots + \$107 \times (1+r)^{-5}$$

Linear interpolation can be used to estimate the yield. Since the current price is higher than $100, r must be lower than 7%.

Initially, try 5% as r:

$7 × 4.3295 [5%, five-year annuity] + $100 × 0.7835 = $30.31 + $78.35 = $108.66

Try 6% as r:
$7 × 4.2124 + $100 × 0.7473 = $29.49 + $74.73 = $104.22

Yield = 5% + (108.66 − 106.62 / 108.66 − 104.22) × 1% = 5.46%

This 5.46% is the YTM of the bond (also known as gross redemption yield). It is the average annual rate of return the bond investors expect to receive from the bond

The yield often quoted in the financial press is the *bid yield*. The bid yield is the YTM for the current bid price (the price at which bonds can be purchased).

©2015 DeVry/Becker Educational Development Corp. All rights reserved.

Term structure of interest rates and the yield curve

The markets demand different yields on bonds with differing lengths of time before their redemption (or maturity), even where the bonds are of the same risk class. This is known as the term structure of interest rates and is represented by the yield curve.

For example, a company may find that if it wants to issue a one-year bond, it may need to pay interest at 3% for the year, if it wants to issue a two-year bond, the markets may demand an annual interest rate of 3.5%, and for a three-year bond the annual yield required may be 4.2%. In this case, the term structure of interest rates is represented by an upward sloping yield curve.

A "normal" yield curve would indeed be upward sloping and is explained by the liquidity preference hypothesis (i.e. investors demand a higher yield to be persuaded to "lock up" their cash for a longer period). In addition the default risk on longer dated corporate bonds may be perceived as higher than on short dated bonds, increasing the upward slope of the yield curve.

However, it is possible for yield curves to be of many different shapes. For example, if there are expectations of falling interest rates in the future the yield curve may become "inversed" (i.e. slop downwards).

Another influence on yield curves is the behaviour of fund managers. Pension fund managers often exhibit a preference for long dated bonds (to match the long-term liabilities of their pension funds). This pushed up the market price of long dated bonds and hence brings down their yield. This is known as the market segmentation theory, sometimes also referred to as the "preferred habitat" theory.

Estimating the spot yield curve

A "spot" interest rate is the rate for borrowing money today to be repaid in a single "bullet" on a specific date in the future. For example, the two year spot rate is the rate for borrowing a sum of money today, paying *zero coupon* over the loan's life, and repaying the principal (plus "rolled up" interest) as a single sum on the loan's maturity date.

Ideally spot interest rates could therefore be directly observed as the quoted yields on zero-coupon bonds. Unfortunately in practice most corporate (and government) bonds tend to pay coupon. In this case spot rates can only be implied through a process known as "boot strapping"

The following example demonstrates how the process works.

Example 3

A government has three bonds in issue that all have a face (par) value of $100 and are redeemable in one year, two years and three years respectively. The bonds are of the same risk class and coupons are payable on an annual basis.

Bond A, which is redeemable in a year's time, has a coupon rate of 7% and is trading at $103.

Bond B, which is redeemable in two years, has a coupon rate of 6% and is trading at $102.

Bond C, which is redeemable in three years, has a coupon rate of 5% and is trading at $98.

To determine the spot yield curve, each bond's cash flows are discounted in turn to determine the annual spot rates as follows:

Bond A: $103 = $107 \times (1 + r_1)^{-1}$
$r_1 = 107/103 - 1 = 0.0388$ or 3.88%

Bond B: $102 = $6 \times 1.0388^{-1} + 106 \times (1 + r_2)^{-2}$
$r_2 = [106 / (102 - 5.78)]^{1/2} - 1 = 0.0496$ or 4.96%

Bond C: $98 = $5 \times 1.0388^{-1} + $5 \times 1.0496^{-2} + 105 \times (1 + r_3)^{-3}$
$r_3 = [105/(98 - 4.81 - 4.54)]^{1/3} - 1 = 0.0580$ or 5.80%

The spot yield curve is therefore:

Year	
1	3.88%
2	4.96%
3	5.80%

Valuing bonds using the spot yield curve

Earlier, in example 1, we valued a bond by discounting each of its future cash flows at the *same* rate (i.e. the YTM).

A technically superior method is to "strip" a bond into its constituent cash flows and discount each cash flow at the spot rate relevant to each strip.

Bond price = Coupon $\times (1 + r_1)^{-1}$ + coupon $\times (1 + r_2)^{-2}$ + ... + coupon $\times (1 + r_n)^{-n}$ + redemption value $\times (1 + r_n)^{-n}$

Where r_1, r_2, etc. are spot interest rates and n is the number of time periods of the coupon.

In this article it is assumed that coupons are paid annually, but in practice coupon is often paid on a semi-annual basis (i.e. half of the coupon is paid every six months).

The financial press and central banks publish estimated spot yield curves based on government issued bonds. Yield curves for individual corporate bonds can be estimated from these by adding the relevant "spread". For example, the following table of spreads (in basis points) is given for the retail sector:

Rating	1 year	2 year	3 year
AAA	14	25	38
AA	29	41	55
A	46	60	76

Example 4

If Mason Retail Co has a credit rating of AA, then its individual spot yield curve – based on the government bond yield curve (from example 3) and the spread table above – may be estimated as:

Year
1 3.88% + 0.29% = 4.17%
2 4.96% + 0.41% = 5.37%
3 5.80% + 0.55% = 6.35%

If Mason issues a three year bond with 5% coupon and $100 par and redemption value, the market price would be:

$5 \times (1.0417)^{-1} + 5 \times (1.0537)^{-2} + 105 \times (1.0635)^{-3} = 96.59$

Linear interpolation could then be used to estimate the yield to maturity

Time	$	6% DF	PV	7% DF	PV
0	(96.59)	1	(96.59)	1	(96.59)
1-3	5	2.673	13.36	2.624	13.12
3	100	0.84	84	0.816	81.60
			0.77		(1.87)

YTM = IRR = 6% + 0.77/(0.77+1.87) = 6.29%

The YTM of 6.29% is slightly lower than the year three spot of 6.35% because some of the returns from the bond come in earlier years, when the interest rates on the yield curve are lower.

Note that the YTM is a weighted average of the spot rates, the weighting being the proportion of returns generated in each year.

INTEREST RATES, BOND AND SWAP VALUATION

Implying forward interest rates

Suppose a bank assesses and quotes the following spot interest rates for a company:

One-year	3.50%
Two-year	4.60%
Three-year	5.40%
Four-year	6.10%
Five-year	6.30%

This indicates that the company would have to pay 3.50% to borrow money today to be repaid as one "bullet" after one year; pay 4.60% to borrow today to be repaid in one bullet after two years; and so on.

Alternatively, for a two-year loan, the company could initially borrow a sum of money for one year at an interest rate of 3.50% and then "rollover" (i.e. refinance the loan from year one to year two).

To hedge its risk the company could request a "forward" interest rate from the bank (i.e. an interest rate agreed today that relates to borrowing money between two dates in the future).

In this case the company would request a 12v24 forward rate agreement (FRA). This fixes the interest rate for borrowing money 12 months from today until 24 months from today.

The question then arises: how may the value of the 12v24 FRA be determined?

Forward rates geometrically "link" spot rates – the 12v24 FRA is effectively a bridge between the one year spot rate and two year spot rate, and can be implied as follows:

The compound factor for the one-year spot rate = 1.035

The compound factor for the two year spot rate = 1.046^2

The one-year forward interest rate can be calculated as follows:
$1.046^2 / 1.0350 = 1.0571$ or 5.71%

Hence the interest rate that applies for borrowing money after one year for a period of one year is 5.71%.

Similarly, forward interest rates can be calculated for other periods in the future:

The 24v36 FRA =
$1.054^3 \div 1.046^2 = 1.0702$ or 7.02%
The 36v48 FRA =
$1.061^4 \div 1.054^3 = 1.0823$ or 8.23%
The 48v60 FRA =
$1.0630^5 \div 1.0610^4 = 1.0710$ or 7.10%

In summary

Year	spot rate	forward rate
1	3.50%	—
2	4.60%	5.71%
3	5.40%	7.02%
4	6.10%	8.23%
5	6.30%	7.10%

Using forward interest rates to value swaps

Suppose the company above has $100m borrowings in the form of variable interest rate loans repayable in five years. It expects interest rates to increase in the future and is therefore keen to fix its interest rate payments.

The bank offers a swap in which the company pays a constant rate of interest to the bank and receives a variable rate from the bank based on the rates above less 50 basis points.

The notional principal in the swap would be $100m.

The amounts of interest the company expects to receive from the bank, based on year 1 spot rate and years 2, 3, 4 and 5 forward rates are:

Year 1   (3.50% − 0.5%) × $100m = $3.00m
Year 2   (5.71% − 0.5%) × $100m = $5.21m
Year 3   (7.02% − 0.5%) × $100m = $6.52m
Year 4   (8.23% − 0.5%) × $100m = $7.73m
Year 5   (7.10% − 0.5%) × $100m = $6.60m

At the start of the swap, the present value of the swap receipts (discounted at spot rates) should equal the present value of the fixed payments to the bank (i.e. the swap should have zero NPV on inception).

If R is the fixed amount of interest the company will pay the bank, then

($3.00m − R) × 1.035^{-1} +
($5.21m − R) × 1.046^{-2} +
($6.52m − R) × 1.054^{-3} +
($7.73m − R) × 1.061^{-4} +
($6.60m − R) × 1.063^{-5}
= 0

2.90m − 0.966R + 4.76m − 0.914R + 5.57m − 0.854R + 6.10m − 0.789R + 4.86m − 0.737R = 0

24.19m − 4.26R = 0
$5.68m = R

As a % = $5.68m/$100m = 5.68%

INTEREST RATES, BOND AND SWAP VALUATION

In practice the receipts and payments of the swap would be netted off (e.g. the company will expect to pay $2.68m ($5.68m – $3.00m) to the bank in year one and expect to receive $0.84m ($6.52m – $5.68m) from the bank in year three). The NPV of all annual flows, discounted at spot rates, will be zero.

The fixed rate of 5.68% is lower than the five-year spot rate of 6.30% because some of the receipts and payments related to the swap contract occur in earlier years when the spot yield curve rate is lower.

Although at the commencement of the contract, the NPV of the swap is zero, as interest rates fluctuate, the value of the swap will change. For example, if interest rates increase and the company pays interest at a fixed rate, then the swap's value to the company will increase.

Tutorial note:

The "plain vanilla" interest rate swap above effectively represents a *series* of FRAs. The fixed rate in the swap should therefore be equivalent in cost to the following series of loans:

✓ initially borrowing the principal for a period of one year;

✓ refinancing the borrowing after one year (i.e. paying the first year's interest and "rolling over" the principal from year one to year two);

✓ rolling over again from year to year three, and so on, until the end of the fifth year when both interest and principal would be repaid.

The cash flows on the above series of loans would be as follows (deducting 50 basis points as previously)

Time	$m
0	100
1	(3)
2	(5.21)
3	(6.52)
4	(7.73)
5	(106.6)

For the fixed rate in the swap to be equivalent in cost it would be set as the IRR of the above cash flows:

Time	$	5% DF	PV	6% DF	PV
0	100	1	100	1	100
1	(3)	0.952	(2.86)	0.943	(2.83)
2	(5.21)	0.907	(4.73)	0.89	(4.64)
3	(6.52)	0.864	(5.63)	0.84	(5.48)
4	(7.73)	0.823	(6.36)	0.792	(6.12)
5	(106.6)	0.784	(83.57)	0.747	(79.63)
			(3.15)		1.30

IRR = 5% + (3.15/3.15+1.30) = 5.71% = swap fixed rate

(rounding difference compared to 5.68%)

BLACK SCHOLES MODEL

This section is based on an article by Patrick Lynch that appeared in "student accountant" but is no longer available on the ACCA website.

The Black Scholes model can be used to calculate the theoretical value of a European-style call option. The value of an option is the premium that must be paid to buy it and is also referred to as the option's price (not to be confused with the exercise/strike price). This article takes a share option as an example.

The five factors that determine option value

The value of an option before expiry	=	**Intrinsic Value** +	**Time Value**
		Current share price	Time period to expiry
		Exercise price	Risk Free interest rate
			Volatility of the share price

Summary of the determinants of option prices

Increase in	**Call**	**Put**
Share Price	Increase	Decrease
Exercise Price	Decrease	Increase
Volatility	Increase	Increase
Time to expiry	Increase	Increase
Interest rate	Increase	Decrease

The Black Scholes model – valuing a call option before the expiry date

Although the formulae are given in the exam you still need to learn the abbreviations and know how to put in the numbers –and bring a scientific calculator!

Call price for a European option:

$$c = P_aN(d_1) - P_eN(d_2)e^{-rt}$$

Where:

$$d_1 = \frac{\ln(P_a/P_e) + \left(r + 0.5s^2\right)t}{s\sqrt{t}}$$

$$d_2 = d_1 - s\sqrt{t}$$

c = price of call option

BLACK SCHOLES MODEL

P_a = price of the underlying asset

$N(d_1)$ = probability that a normal distribution is less than d_1 standard deviations above the mean

P_e = exercise price/strike price

r = annual risk free interest rate

t = time to expiry (in years)

s = annual standard deviation of the underlying asset's returns

e = the exponential constant

ln = the natural log (log to the base e)

Put – Call Parity Theorem

value of a put = value of a call – current share price + present value of exercise price.

$p = c - P_a + P_e e^{-rt}$

Where:

P = price of put option

$P_e e^{-rt}$ = present value of the exercise price

Limitations of the Black Scholes Model

The model assumes:

1. options are European calls.
2. no transaction costs or taxes.
3. investor can borrow at the risk free rate.
4. risk free rate of interest is constant and the share's volatility is constant over the life of the option.
5. future share price volatility can be estimated by observing past share price volatility.
6. share price movements follow the standard normal distribution.
7. no dividends are payable before the option expiry date (although it is straightforward to modify the model for European options to take this into account)

Variants on the Black Scholes Model

Since the original model was published it has been developed into other applications. For example:

✓ the Merton model (see next section) – which values equity as a European call option over a firm's assets, the strike price being the level of liabilities;

✓ valuation of "real options" embedded within corporate projects (e.g. valuing an abandonment option as a European put option – although such options are often closer to American style and more accurately valued using binomial models);

✓ valuation of intangible assets (e.g. owning a patent can be viewed as a having a call option on a project).

"THE GREEKS"

Delta

Delta is the change in the price of an option compared to a change in the price of the underlying asset.

$$\text{Delta D} = N(d_1) = \frac{\text{Change in the option price}}{\text{Change in share price}}$$

Change of call price with change in share price

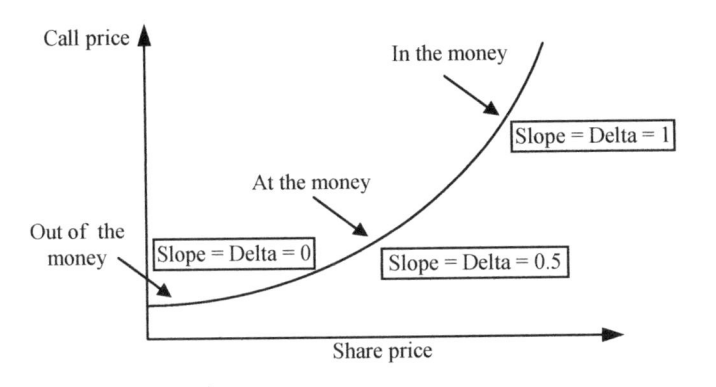

A put option has a negative delta (i.e. the price of a put moves in the opposite direction to the movement in the share price). The delta for put options is calculated as $N(d_1) - 1$ and is between 0 and -1.

Delta Hedging

An investor who holds a number of shares and sells/writes a number of call options in the proportion dictated by delta ensures a hedged portfolio. A hedged portfolio is one where the gains and losses cancel each other out. For this reason delta is also referred to as the hedge ratio.

$$\text{Number of option calls to sell} = \frac{\text{Number of shares bought}}{N(d1)}$$

Delta is the gradient/slope of the graph above. However delta is not a constant – the slope is not linear. The portfolio will need rebalancing as the delta value changes – referred to as dynamic hedging. The frequency of this depends on the rate of change of delta, measured by gamma.

Gamma (G)

- ✓ Gamma measures the rate of change of delta (the sensitivity of delta) as the share price changes.

$$\text{Gamma} = \frac{\text{Change in delta}}{\text{Change in share price}}$$

- ✓ Gamma is the rate of change of the slope in the graph above.

- ✓ Gamma is high when an option is at, or close to, the money.

- ✓ Gamma is low when an option is deep in the money, or deep out of the money.

Theta (q) – Time

- ✓ the time value of all options reduces over time towards zero. The theta measures how much value is lost over time. The theta is usually expressed as the amount of loss per day.

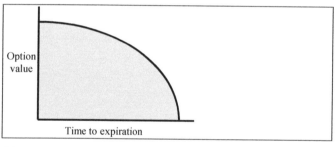

Vega – Volatility

- ✓ Vega measures how much option prices change with changes in share price volatility. It is always positive and therefore as price volatility increases the option premium (for puts or calls) will always increase.

BLACK SCHOLES MODEL

Rho (r) – Interest Rate

✓ Measures how much option prices change with changes in the risk free interest rate.

✓ If interest rates rise the value of call options also rises as the holder of a call option does not have to pay the exercise price until the expiry date. If interest rates are high the value of deferring payment is high.

✓ If interest rate rise the value of put options falls as the holder has to wait to receive the exercise price. If interest rates are high the present value of future receipts is low.

Summary of Greeks

	Change in	*Regarding*
Delta	Option value	Share Price
Gamma	Delta	Share Price
Theta	Option Value	Time
Vega	Option Value	Volatility
Rho	Option Value	Interest Rate

MERTON MODEL

This section is based on an article by Professor Bob Ryan which appeared in "student accountant" but is no longer available on the ACCA website.

*Note – the paper P4 syllabus demands an appreciation of the Merton model – calculations will **not** be required.*

Robert Merton worked with Black and Scholes on their original model for pricing financial options. He later applied the model to company valuation for situations where conventional techniques cannot be used, or where they do not fully reflect the risks involved.

Merton viewed shareholders as having a call option over the firm's assets, with the exercise price being the value of the firm's liabilities.

Due to limited liability the shareholders are not liable for their firm's debts in the event of default. If, when the debt matures, the value of assets is greater than the value of the debt (A–L in **Figure 1**), then the equity shareholders are entitled to the difference. If the value of the assets falls below the value of the debt, the firm can liquidate the business and shareholders walk away.

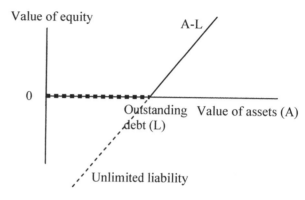

Figure 1: The payoff on limited versus unlimited liability

In **Table 1** we translate the generic variables for the Black Scholes model into what must be measured when valuing corporate equity as a call option.

MERTON MODEL

Table 1

Value of underlying asset	Value in use of assets
Volatility of the underlying asset	Standard deviation of asset value
Exercise price	Redemption value of outstanding debt
Time to expiry	Term to maturity of debt
Risk-free rate	Risk-free rate over the term of the firm's debt

In the case of a bank, the majority of assets may be actively traded and hence the fair value in the balance sheet should represent their economic value. In the case of other companies, value in use should be the present value of the future cash flows that the assets are expected to generate over their useful lives.

The volatility of asset value is probably the most difficult variable to estimate accurately. One approach is to simulate the expected future cash flows of the business, generating a distribution of present values from which the volatility can be obtained.

For simplicity Merton assumed that the firm had issued debt in the form of a single, zero coupon bond. In practice, firms issue debt of various types, many of which provide a return in the form of interest as well as redemption value. The easiest approach to find the effective exercise price of the shareholders' call option is via the following steps:

1 Estimate the average term to maturity of the company's outstanding long-term debt.

2 Estimate the average coupon interest rate.

3 Use the YTM on the firm's debt (this could be the quoted rate on any variable debt in issue or the yield given for the firm's credit rating) to estimate the market value of a notional $100 bond.

4 Estimate the repayment value of an equivalent zero-coupon bond.

Note that under IFRS, the company's debt may be shown at fair value and so steps 2 and 3 would not be required.

Example

A company has $100 face value of debt in issue carrying 5% coupon interest and five years to maturity. The company's current cost of debt is 8%.

The market value of the debt is estimated as follows:

Year	1	2	3	4	5
Cash flow	5	5	5	5	105
8% DF	0.926	0.857	0.794	0.735	0.681
Present value	4.63	4.29	3.97	3.68	71.51
Market value	$88				

The redemption value of an equivalent zero coupon bond is calculated by finding the future value which, when discounted at 8% over five years, gives a present value of $88.

$88 = FV \times 0.681$

$FV = \$129$

Hence the exercise price would be set at $129 and the time to expiry as 5 years

An alternative approach is to calculate the weighted average term to maturity of the bond's cash flows – known as Macaulay duration:

Year	1	2	3	4	5
Cash flow	5	5	5	5	105
8% DF	0.926	0.857	0.794	0.735	0.681
Present value	4.63	4.29	3.97	3.68	71.51
Year × PV	4.63	8.58	11.91	14.72	357.55
Total	397				

$$\text{Duration} = \frac{397}{88} = 4.5 \text{ years}$$

In this case the time to expiry would be set at 4.5 years and the exercise price as the total payment on the debt (i.e. 5 + 5 + 5 + 5 + 105 = $125). The exercise price is set slightly lower than in the zero-coupon method, increasing the intrinsic value of the call option, but the time to expiry is set slightly shorter, giving a commensurate reduction in the time value.

Overall both methods of calibrating the firm's debt should give similar results when valuing the firm's equity.

Practical application

Let us apply the Merton model to the distressed UK bank, Northern Rock. In March 2007, the company reported assets and liabilities at fair value of £113.2bn and £110.7bn respectively. (**Tutorial note:** *presumably the author has calibrated the fair value of debt to its effective redemption value*).

The average term to maturity on the bank's liabilities was approximately 100 days. This is not unusual for a bank whose liabilities are in the form of short-term money market borrowing and deposits. At that point, the risk free rate of interest was 3.5%.

The value of an option rises with the level of risk, and this is particularly the case when the option is "near the money" (i.e. where the underlying asset value is close to the strike price). In the context of the Merton model this is where assets are close to liabilities, as in the case of Northern Rock. Taking two test values, of 5% and 10%, for the volatility of the bank's assets, the model gives the following valuation:

Volatility (s)	5%	10%
Firm asset value (£bn)	113.20	113.20
Liability value (£bn)	110.70	110.70
Risk free rate	0.035	0.035
Time to exercise (days)	100	100

d_1	1.16474	0.60609
d_2	1.13312	0.54284
$N(d_1)$	0.87794	0.72777
$N(d_2)$	0.87142	0.70638
Equity value (£bn)	4.26	5.27
Share price (£)	8.59	10.64

Tutorial note: *$N(d_2)$ measures the probability that the option will be exercised on expiry. In this context it measures the probability that the value of assets will exceed the level of debt on its maturity date. Therefore $1 - N(d2)$ measures the probability that the value of assets will be below the level of debt, in which case the firm would default.*

In fact, the share price of the bank in March 2007 was around £9.50 per share (based on 495.6m shares in issue).

Let's see what happens if the asset value falls to £110.7bn. On the statement of financial position the value of the firm's equity should be zero. However, the Merton model gives a quite different result. At a volatility of 5%, the equity is still worth £2.29bn or £4.62 per share – almost exactly its value in September 2007. In **Figure 2** below we can see how the value of the bank's equity is predicted to change with changing asset value.

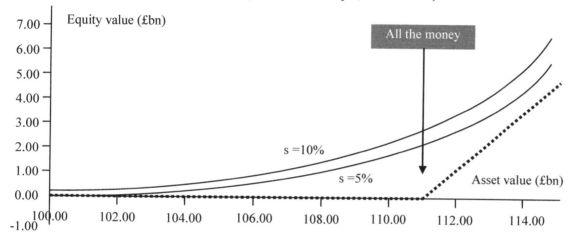

Figure 2: Equity value versus asset value (Northern Rock plc, March 2007)

How can equity still have substantial positive value even though the balance sheet shows a nil balance on a fair value basis? The answer is that limited liability protects the equity investors from loss, and indeed they have everything to gain if the asset value should recover.

This leads us to another interesting revelation – when a firm is" near the money" (i.e. when its level of gearing approaches 100%) the equity investors will develop an appetite for risk. They will therefore incentivise management to take risk rather than reduce it – leading to the high levels of rewards paid to bank staff and particularly to those in the risk-taking part of the business.

Tutorial note: *the bankers themselves also have a form of protection in that their bonuses cannot be negative if their gambles fail*

It was only when the threat of nationalisation became an issue in the last months of 2007 that the equity value of Northern Rock started to collapse, and this is also easily explained within the Merton framework.

Nationalisation has the effect of eliminating the chance of asset recovery for the shareholders, effectively depriving them of the time value of their call option on the underlying assets of the business.

Conclusion

Merton provides a framework for the valuation of companies that are financed, in part, by borrowing. Where shareholders are protected by limited liability they have a call option on the underlying assets of the business. Using the Merton model, we can estimate the value of a firm's equity on the basis of the value of its assets and their volatility.

For companies that are "deep in the money" the time value will be relatively small and intrinsic value (i.e. the present value of assets less liabilities) will dominate the value of equity. In this situation, normal risk aversion will apply as the intrinsic value will be equally exposed to both positive and negative movements in the values of the firm's assets.

The situation changes dramatically with companies that are "near the money". This can occur with high growth start-ups financed by debt, leveraged buyouts, and indeed companies that are at risk of default.

However, one class of company – banks – almost always operate near the money. In valuing such businesses, time value will be more important than intrinsic value. When time value dominates the equity investors become risk aggressive, as the more risk that is taken by management the greater the value of equity. As a result a bank will incentivise its management to take risk.

This section is based on an article by the examiner. The original article appeared in "student accountant" and can be found at http://www.accaglobal.co.uk/en/student/acca-qual-student-journey/qual-resource/acca-qualification/p4/technical-articles.html

Understanding why is as important as understanding how

It is important that students understand *why* corporations manage risk. Risk management costs money but does it actually add more value to a corporation?

Risk refers to the volatility of returns (both positive and negative) that can be quantified through measures such as probabilities, standard deviations and correlations. Its management is about changing the volatility of returns a corporation is exposed to (e.g. changing exposure to floating interest rates by swapping them to fixed rates).

Management must decide which projects to undertake, how they should be financed and whether the volatility of a project's returns should be managed.

The volatility of returns should be managed if it results in increasing value. Given that the market value of a corporation is the NPV of its future cash flows discounted by the return required by its investors, then higher market value can either be generated by increasing the future cash flows or by reducing investors' required rate of return (or both).

The return required by investors is the sum of the risk free rate and a premium for the risk they face. If investors hold well-diversified portfolios of investments then they are only exposed to systematic risk as their exposure to firm-specific risk has been diversified away. Therefore the risk premium of their required return is based on the capital asset pricing model (CAPM).

Research suggests companies with a wide shareholder base do not increase value by diversifying company specific risk, as their equity holders have already achieved this level of risk diversification. Moreover, risk management activity designed to reduce *systematic* risk would not be worthwhile because, in perfect markets, the benefits achieved from risk management would equal the costs.

This argument would not apply to smaller companies which have non-diversified equity investors. In this case the equity holders are exposed to both specific and systematic risk and would benefit from risk diversification by the company.

However research has found that risk management is undertaken mostly by larger companies with diverse equity holdings and not by the smaller companies. The reason is that the costs related to risk management are large and mostly fixed. Small companies simply cannot afford these costs nor can they benefit from the economies of scale that large companies can achieve.

RISK MANAGEMENT

In addition to the ability of larger companies to undertake risk management, market imperfections may provide the motivation for them to do so. The following discussion considers the circumstances which may result in providing such opportunities.

Taxation

Where a corporation faces a progressive tax system a reduction in the variability of earnings may keep the firm in a lower tax bracket.

Insolvency and financial distress

A corporation is insolvent when it cannot meet its financial obligations as they fall due.

Financial distress is where a corporation can operate on a day-to-day basis, but it finds that these operations are difficult to conduct because the parties dealing with it are concerned that it may become insolvent in the future. When facing financial distress a corporation will incur additional costs, both direct and indirect.

The main indirect costs of financial distress relate to the higher costs of contracting with the corporation's stakeholders (e.g. customers, employees and suppliers).

Customers may demand better warranty schemes; employees may demand higher salaries; senior management may ask for "golden hellos" before agreeing to join the corporation; and suppliers may be unwilling to offer favourable credit terms.

As such stakeholders face the corporation's *total* risk (as opposed to just the systematic risk faced by its shareholders) they demand greater compensation for their participation.

Where an organisation actively manages its risk and prevents situations of financial distress, it will find it easier to contract with its stakeholders and at a lower cost.

External funding and agency costs

Financial distress may make the cost of external debt and equity so expensive that a corporation may be forced to reject profitable projects.

Equity investors in effect hold a call option on a corporation's assets, the strike price being the amount they would need to cancel the firm's debts (for more detail refer to the *Merton Model*). In cases of low financial distress the call option may be considered to be "at-the-money" for the equity holders. In this case shareholders are willing to undertake risky projects as they would benefit from any increase in profitability, but the impact of any loss is restricted due to the protection of limited liability.

©2015 DeVry/Becker Educational Development Corp. All rights reserved.

However when raising debt capital, a corporation that is subject to low levels of financial distress would face higher agency costs – with lenders imposing higher borrowing costs and more restrictive covenants. Debt holders get a fixed return on their investment; any additional benefit due to higher profits would go to the equity holders. This would make the debt holders reluctant to allow the corporation to undertake risky projects or to lend more finance to the corporation.

In the case of substantial financial distress, the call option could be considered to be "out-of-the money". In this situation there is little benefit to equity holders of undertaking new projects, as the benefits of these will first pass to the debt holders (although debt holders would be reluctant to lend to a severely distressed company in any case).

A corporation that faces high levels of financial distress would find it difficult to raise equity capital in order to undertake new investments. If corporations try to raise equity finance for relatively less risky projects then the profits earned from such projects would initially go to the debt holders and the equity holders will gain only residual profits. Therefore equity holders would put pressure on the corporation to reject good, low risk projects, which may have been acceptable to the bondholders.

Therefore, risk management to reduce financial distress may help the firm to obtain an optimal mix of debt and equity, and to undertake profitable projects.

Capital structure and information asymmetry

Risk management can help a corporation obtain an optimal capital structure of debt and equity to maximise its value. Since risk management reduces the volatility of cash flows this enables a corporation to take more debt finance in its capital structure. Since debt is cheaper than external equity (due to lower required return and the tax shield) taking on more debt should increase the value of the corporation.

"Pecking order theory" states that in practice managers actually prefer to use *internally* generated funds rather than going to the external markets. Borrowing from the external markets, whether equity or debt, involves parties who do not have complete information about the corporation. This information asymmetry makes external sources of funds more expensive.

If risk management stabilises the cash flows that the corporation receives from year to year, then this would enable managers to plan when the necessary internal funds will become available for future investments with greater accuracy. They will then be able to align their investment policies with the availability of funding.

RISK MANAGEMENT

Manager behaviour towards risk management

Managers whose reward structure includes large equity stakes are more likely to reduce the corporation's risk compared to managers whose reward structure is based on equity options.

Managers who hold concentrated equity stakes in a corporation face higher levels of risk when compared to external shareholders. As discussed previously, investors hold well-diversified portfolios and face exposure to systematic risk only. But managers with concentrated equity stakes would face both systematic and unsystematic risk. Therefore, they have a motivation to reduce the unsystematic risk.

However investors do not reward corporations that are reducing unsystematic risk; because they have diversified this risk away themselves. If managers use the corporation's resources to reduce unsystematic risk they thereby reduce the corporation's value. On the other hand it could be argued that if managers are allowed to diversify their firm's unsystematic risk they are then free to focus on improving the firm's performance, although whether this can be justified on a cost/benefit analysis is doubtful.

So why do managers not simply diversify the risk of concentrated equity investments themselves? They could sell their shares and build a wide personal portfolio.

Research has found that senior managers are reluctant to reduce their concentrated equity positions because any attempt to sell the equity would send negative signals to the markets.

Managers who own equity *options,* which can be converted into equity at a future date, will actively seek to *increase* the risk of a corporation rather than reduce it. Managers who hold equity options are interested in maximising the future price of the equity. Therefore they will be more inclined to undertake risky projects (and less inclined to manage risk). Equity options, as a form of reward, have been often criticised because they do not necessarily make managers behave in the best interests of the corporation or its equity investors, but encourage them to act in an overly risky manner.

Testing the impact of risk management

The main finding from research is that: corporations manage their risks in the belief that this would create or increase corporate value, although a direct link between risk management and a corresponding increase in corporate value has not been established.

©2015 DeVry/Becker Educational Development Corp. All rights reserved.

HOW LENDERS SET THEIR RATES

This section is based on an article by Professor Bob Ryan; the original article is no longer available on the ACCA website.

It is just as important to understand how the debt market works as it is to understand the operation of the equity market. This article explores the ways in which lenders decide the rate they will charge against any particular loan.

With equity, capital asset pricing theory tells us that a firm's exposure to market risk is the principal determinant of a firm's equity cost of capital. With debt, market risk is not so important – what is important is whether a borrower will default on a loan. This is credit risk – a separate class of risk.

Default occurs when the value of a borrower's assets falls below the value of their outstanding debt. Therefore, two variables influence the potential loss to the lender: the chance of default occurring, and the part of the debt that can then be recovered by the sale of the firm's assets.

If the probability of a company defaulting is 5%, and only 80% of the debt can be recovered by the lender (that is, 20% will be lost), then at least an extra 1% (20% × 5%) will be charged to cover the potential loss. It's not as simple as this in practice because the lender loses not only part of the sum advanced but also the accrued interest.

For the largest loans, or where the borrower is considering a bond issue, then the borrower itself will need to obtain a credit risk assessment from a rating agency such as Moody's, Standard and Poor's, or Fitch.

Two approaches to credit risk assessment

The first approach involves collecting financial and other measures. In 1966 William Beaver in 1966 identified which of the common accounting ratios had the highest predictive value in assessing bankruptcy risk. He showed that one ratio – operating cash flow divided by total outstanding debt – successfully predicted default within five years with better than 70% accuracy. Edward Altman in the US, and Richard Taffler in the UK, developed more sophisticated multivariate models. Other models, such as that developed by Robert Kaplan and Gabriel Urwitz, focus on explaining the credit ratings given by the agencies. However, a common criticism of all these models is that they have weak theoretical support and detailed knowledge is not examinable.

The second approach is based on what are called "structural models". Structural models rely on an assessment of the underlying riskiness of a firm's assets or its cash generation, and the likelihood the firm will not be able to pay interest or repay capital on the due date.

Estimating the credit risk premium for the risk neutral lender

Take a firm that has assets with a current value of $1m and outstanding debt of $0.4m. The volatility of those assets (as given by the standard deviation of monthly asset values) is 10.23%. We can calculate the probability that within the next 12 months the assets will fall in value to less than $0.4m, thereby triggering default.

A 10.23% monthly (σ_m) volatility can be converted to an annual volatility (σ_a) as follows:

$$\sigma_a = \sigma_m \times \sqrt{T}$$

where T is the number of time periods (months in a year). Therefore:

$$\sigma_a = 10.23\% \times \sqrt{12} = 35.44\%$$

which, when applied to an average asset value of $1m, gives a standard deviation of $354,400.

The "distance to default" in value = $1m – $0.4m = $0.6m. Dividing this by the standard deviation tells by how many standard deviations the asset value must fall to trigger default.

Statistics refers to the number of standard deviations as a "Z score".

$$Z = \frac{\text{fall in value to default}}{\text{standard deviation}} = \frac{\$600,000}{\$354,400} = 1.693$$

Using standard normal distribution tables (published in the exam) we can see that the proportion represented by 1.693 standard deviations is 0.4548. Adding this to the probability of an asset value being above the mean (0.5) gives a total probability of not defaulting of 0.9548 (i.e. a probability of defaulting of 0.0452).

The second part of the default assessment is to estimate the potential "recoverability" of the debt. A number of issues influence recoverability such as:

✓ the nature of the firm's assets and their saleability;
✓ any covenants which impose restrictions on their disposal;
✓ the priority of the lender; and
✓ any directors' guarantees that may be in place.

We can then work towards an estimate of the "default spread" that a bank will charge for a loan. Assume it assesses the recoverability of the debt as 80% and that it, in turn, pays LIBOR of 5% to raise finance. On a loan of $400,000, the bank would expect to receive LIBOR plus the premium it wishes to charge at the end of the year, giving an overall rate of i%.

A simple decision tree shows how the bank equates the present value of a certain sum of $400,000 to the uncertain future outcomes on the loan:

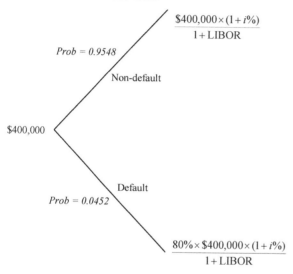

Either the lender receives its principal sum back, plus interest at i%, or it receives just 80% of that value. We have discounted at LIBOR on the assumption that the lender is neutral towards risk – an assumption we will relax later.

We can express this decision tree as a simple equation:

$$\$400{,}000 = 0.9548 \times \frac{\$400{,}000 \times (1+i)}{1.05} + 0.0452 \times \frac{0.8 \times \$400{,}000 \times (1+i)}{1.05}$$

re-arranging

$$i = \frac{1.05}{0.9548 + 0.0452 \times 0.8} - 1 = 0.0596$$

or 5.96%, which is 96 basis points credit spread over LIBOR.

Adjusting the rate for risk aversion

Banks, however, are not neutral towards risk. The potential loss of 20% of the loan is more significant to them than the potential gain if the lender remains solvent. To compensate, a bank will add a percentage to the discount rate to cover its aversion to risk, and any other charges it may wish to make. If we assume, in this case, that the lender requires an additional 50 basis points (0.5%) then the previous calculation becomes:

$$\$400{,}000 = 0.9548 \times \frac{\$400{,}000 \times (1+i)}{1.055} + 0.0452 \times$$

$$\frac{0.8 \times \$400{,}000 \times (1+i)}{1.055}$$

re-arranging

$$i = \frac{1.055}{0.9548 + 0.0452 \times 0.8} - 1 = 0.0646$$

which gives a rate of 6.46%.

A problem with this type of analysis is how to estimate the asset value of the firm and the volatility of that asset value.

The solution may come from options pricing theory. A call option is an option for the holder to purchase an asset at a set price on or before a set date. In a limited liability company partly financed by debt, equity investors can "walk away" in the event that the value of the firm's assets is less than the amount borrowed. Alternatively, if there is surplus asset value they have the option to redeem the debt and take the difference. Hence the value of the firm's equity can be viewed as the value of a call option on the underlying assets of the business.

In 1974 Merton developed the Black Scholes model into a format for valuing equity as a European call option where:

✓ the exercise price is the redemption value of debt

✓ time to expiry is the years to redemption of debt (for simplicity Merton assumed the debt to be a zero coupon bond with one year to redemption at face value)

✓ the value of the underlying asset is the market value of the firm's assets.

✓ volatility is the volatility of the asset value.

For a quoted company we can directly observe the value of the firm's equity (i.e. the output from Merton's valuation model). The value of assets and their volatility can then be mathematically derived.

Tutorial note: *an alternative formulation of the structural debt model is to estimate the probability that the firm will not have enough cash to pay all the interest on the debt during the next year. Hence the "distance to default" represents the fall in post-interest cash flow to zero, and the Z-score found by comparing to the volatility of this cash flow. From that point all other calculations are as before. Question 3 of the December 2008 exam uses this approach.*

This section is based on an article by Professor Bob Ryan. The original article appeared in "student accountant" and can be found at http://www.accaglobal.co.uk/en/student/acca-qual-student-journey/qual-resource/acca-qualification/p4/technical-articles.html

IRR

Compared with NPV the IRR has many drawbacks:

✖   it is only a relative measure of value creation;

✖   it can have multiple solutions;

✖   it appears to make a reinvestment assumption that is unrealistic (i.e. that returns from a project can be reinvested at the IRR itself).

However financial managers like IRR as a percentage measure of project performance; it provides a useful tool to measure "headroom" when negotiating with suppliers of funds.

So is there a better measure which keeps the benefits of IRR without the drawbacks?

Modified Internal Rate of Return (MIRR)

This is a similar technique to IRR. Technically, it is the IRR for a project with an identical level of investment and NPV to that being considered but with a single terminal cash inflow.

Example 1

A project requires an initial investment of $1,000, and offers cash returns of $400, $500, and $300 at the end of years one, two and three respectively. The company's cost of capital is 10%.

	Year				
	0	1	2	3	NPV	IRR
Project cash flow ($)	-1,000.00	400.00	600.00	300.00		
Discounted cash flow ($)	-1,000.00	363.64	495.87	225.39	84.90	14.92%

The project is viable in NPV terms, and this is also reflected in the IRR which is greater than the firm's cost of capital of 10%.

There are two methods we can use for calculating MIRR

MODIFIED INTERNAL RATE OF RETURN

Method 1

Stage 1: Take the cash flows from the return phase (i.e. year one onwards in this example) and compound each cash flow forward to the end of the project using the firm's cost of capital.

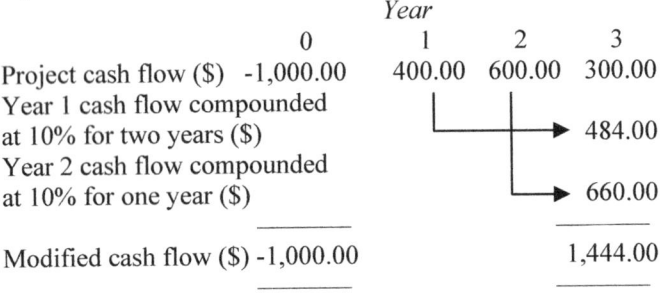

	Year		
0	1	2	3
Project cash flow ($) -1,000.00	400.00	600.00	300.00
Year 1 cash flow compounded at 10% for two years ($)			484.00
Year 2 cash flow compounded at 10% for one year ($)			660.00
Modified cash flow ($) -1,000.00			1,444.00

Note we have a modified cash flow which has an identical NPV to the original project.

Stage 2: Taking the total of the cash flows extended to year three, calculate the discount rate required to set this value, when discounted, equal to the outlay. To do this we need to use the following formula:

$$\text{Outlay} = \frac{\text{Terminal cash flow}}{(1 + \text{MIRR})^n}$$

n is the number of years of the project. We can rearrange this formula and find a solution for this project as follows:

$$\text{MIRR} = \sqrt[n]{\frac{\text{Terminal cash flow}}{\text{Outlay}}} - 1$$

$$\text{MIRR} = \sqrt[3]{\frac{1444}{1000}} - 1 = 13.03\%$$

The only problem with this method is that it is time consuming to perform.

Method 2

$$\text{MIRR} = \sqrt[n]{\left(\frac{PV}{\text{Outlay}}\right)} \times (1+i) - 1$$

Take the present value (PV) of the cash flows from the return/recovery phase (not the NPV), divide by the outlay and take the "nth" root of the result. Multiply the result by one plus the cost of capital (1.1 in this case), deduct one and you have the answer.

Therefore

$$\text{MIRR} = \sqrt[3]{\left(\frac{1084.90}{1000}\right)} \times (1.1) - 1 = 13.03\%$$

More complex projects

The most common complication is where the investment phase stretches over a number of years. To handle this type of problem we divide the cash flows from the project into an "investment" phase and a "return" phase.

Take a project which has an investment phase of 12 months which consists of an initial investment of $700 and a further investment of $300 one year later. At the end of the second year, the project is expected to commence the return phase with a cash return of $400, followed by $600 and $300 in years three and four respectively. As before, we will assume a 10% cost of capital as the discount rate.

	Investment phase		Return phase		
	0	1	2	3	4
Project cash flow	-700.00	-300.00	400.00	600.00	300.00
Modified cash flow	-700.00	-272.73	484.00	660.00	300.00
PV of investment phase	-972.73				
Future value of return phase					1,444.00
PV of return phase	986.27		330.58	450.79	204.90

The IRR of this project is 10.59%.

Using method 1, the modified cash flow is calculated by *discounting* the investment phase at 10% to give a PV of capital investment of $972.73 and *compounding* the return phase to a terminal cash flow gives $1,444.00. The MIRR is calculated as follows, but this time for a four-year project:

$$MIRR = \sqrt[n]{\frac{\text{Terminal cash flow}}{\text{Outlay}}} - 1$$

$$MIRR = \sqrt[4]{\frac{1444}{972.73}} - 1 = 10.38\%$$

Alternatively, method 2 gives the same result, but is more efficient given that the PV of the project is usually calculated anyway as part of an investment appraisal exercise:

$$MIRR = \sqrt[n]{\left(\frac{\text{PV of return phase}}{\text{PV of investment phase}}\right)} \times (1+i) - 1$$

$$MIRR = \sqrt[4]{\frac{986.27}{972.73}} \times (1.1) - 1 = 10.38\%$$

Using this formula, MIRR is quicker to calculate than IRR.

MODIFIED INTERNAL RATE OF RETURN

MIRR is invariably lower than IRR and some would argue that it makes a more realistic assumption about the reinvestment rate.

Traditional IRR assumes the cash flows generated by a project are reinvested within the project itself. However in practice they are often reinvested elsewhere within the firm or paid as a dividend and it is not a fair assumption that the firm or its shareholders is capable of generating that IRR on other investments.

MIRR is also a unique answer whereas traditional IRR can be a multiple solution particularly if there are cash out flows at the end of the project (e.g. decommissioning costs).

However MIRR still suffers from the limitation of being a relative measure – as a % it does not show the $ change in shareholder wealth.

Published formula

$$MIRR = \left[\frac{PV_R}{PV_I} \right]^{\frac{1}{n}} (1 + r_e) - 1$$

PV_R = *present value of the project's returns*
PV_I = *present value of the investment outlay*
n = *number of years*
r_e = *reinvestment rate (i.e. cost of capital)*

SHARE BUYBACKS

This section is based on an article by Peter Atrill which is no longer available on the ACCA website.

A share buyback occurs when a business purchases its own shares and then either cancels them or holds them as treasury stock for re-issue at a later date. Microsoft Corporation announced, in September 2008, its intention to buy back $40bn worth of its own shares over a five-year period.

A business may acquire its shares:

- ✓ in the open market; or
- ✓ by a proportional offer, where a set proportion from each investor is purchased; or
- ✓ by a tender offer, where a fixed number of shares are acquired at a particular price.

Buybacks versus dividends

If we assume perfect capital markets shareholders will be indifferent between a buyback and a dividend.

Example 1

Yen plc has one million shares in issue, and surplus cash of £2m which is to be distributed to investors. Following this distribution, profits are expected to be £1m per year, and the price/earnings ratio is expected to be eight.

The distribution will be made by either a dividend of £2 per share, or a tender offer of 200,000 shares at £10 per share.

Whichever distribution method is chosen, the total market value (TMV) of the shares will be the same, as the risks will be unaffected by the choice of method. :

TMV = profit $\times$ p/e ratio = £1m $\times$ 8 = £8m.

Under the dividend option, however, there will be one million shares in issue, and under the buyback option there will be 800,000 shares in issue. This means that the value per share will be £8 (£8m/1m) under the dividend option and £10 (£8m/800,000) under the buyback option.

SHARE BUYBACKS

Consider a shareholder with 10,000 shares:

	Dividend option	Buyback option	
		Hold	Sell
	£	£	£
10,000 shares held at £8 per share	80,000		
10,000 shares held at £10 per share		100,000	
10,000 shares sold at £10 per share			100,000
Dividend received (10,000 x £2)	20,000		
Wealth	100,000	100,000	100,000

In practice there are various reasons why a share buyback may be preferred:

Flexibility

Managers are unlikely to respond to a temporary cash surplus by increasing dividends as this raises investor expectations of the same, or even higher, level in future. Share buybacks, on the other hand, tend to be regarded by investors as a distribution of surplus cash in a particular year.

Postponing, or even abandoning, a share buyback programme does not incur the kind of adverse reaction from investors that would normally accompany a cut in dividends.

Where a programme of open market purchases over a period of time is adopted, managers have considerable discretion over the timing and amount of shares purchased. There is much less discretion, however, where a tender offer or proportional offer is adopted.

Taxation

Any gains arising from the sale of shares will be subject to capital gains tax. In some countries, the taxation rules treat capital gains differently to dividends (e.g. in the UK, capital gains below a certain threshold are not taxable, but all dividends are taxable). Furthermore, it is possible for an investor to the timing of capital gains by choosing when to sell shares, whereas the timing of dividends normally rests with the managers of the business.

If buybacks are made on a regular and frequent basis, however, the tax authorities may conclude that their purpose is simply to avoid taxation: this runs the risk that they will be treated for tax purposes as dividends.

Undervalued shares

Where share values are temporarily depressed, open market purchases will benefit investors who continue to hold their shares. The purchase of shares below their fair value will transfer wealth from those investors that sell to those that continue to hold. Critics argue that this is unfair to the investors that sell. Instead, a proportional offer, or tender offer, where shares are purchased at a premium to their current value, would provide a more equitable way to return funds.

Market signalling

Managers have access to information that investors do not have – asymmetry of information. Whereas investors may by cynical of bullish statements and favourable predictions, concrete actions (e.g. share buybacks or increased dividends) are likely to be taken more seriously.

To alter the capital structure

A recent survey of finance directors of the top 200 UK businesses found that achieving an optimal capital structure (i.e. minimised WACC) was the main reason cited for undertaking share buybacks.

In November 2007 Siemens announced an intention to optimise its capital structure and simultaneously announced a share repurchase programme of up to €10bn to achieve this.

Returning surplus funds

Where a business has no profitable opportunities in which to invest, returning any surplus funds may be the best option for investors (i.e. a residual distribution policy).

More mature, low-growth businesses are likely to find themselves in this position than younger, high-growth businesses.

Reducing agency costs

There is a risk that managers will use the resources of the business unwisely, perhaps in ways that benefit themselves rather than investors – the resulting loss in shareholder wealth is referred to as agency costs. To prove their integrity managers may decide to distribute any temporary cash surplus to investors through a share buyback.

Agency costs may also be reduced where a share buyback is used to alter the capital structure of the business. If debt capital is substituted for equity capital, the increase in interest payments that occurs will subject managers to much tighter financial discipline, as it will reduce the discretionary funds available.

However the following two examples show that share buybacks are sometimes carried out to benefit the managers rather than investors:

Increasing earnings per share

Where a business has surplus funds, buying back shares will result in an increase in earnings per share. As this measure is often used in managers' long-term incentive plans, there is a risk that managers will use a share buyback in order to boost their rewards.

Increasing earnings per share is not the same as increasing shareholder value. EPS is influenced by accounting policy choices and fails to take account of the cost of capital and future cash flows, which are the determinants of value.

Management share options

Following a dividend payment, the share price will decrease and will be lower than the share price following a share buyback. Managers with share options therefore have an incentive to employ buybacks rather than dividend payments.

The market does not react as well to buyback announcements from businesses with significant management share option schemes.

The United Kingdom Shareholders' Association (UKSA), which represents the interests of private investors, has argued that a buyback announcement should be accompanied by a clear explanation of the reasons for a buyback and its likely effect on future profits, capital structure and dividends. The particular method of buyback should also be justified. UKSA further argues that the annual report should set out a detailed account of any share buybacks, along with a report by the directors on the extent to which the buyback programme has achieved its objectives.

Summary

In a world of perfect markets, it will not matter whether funds are returned to investors through a share buyback or through a dividend payment.

In an imperfect world, however, financial flexibility and taxation considerations may favour a share buyback. While share buybacks may be used to enhance the value of an investor's shares, they can also be abused for non-value-enhancing purposes. Investors must be alert to this risk and should closely scrutinise share buyback proposals. To help them in this task, much fuller disclosure is required.

Share buybacks have become a very popular method of returning funds to investors. During 2007, it was estimated that nearly 15% of Europe's large and mid-cap businesses carried out buybacks of more than 2% of their market capitalisation.

This section is based on an article by Steve Jay but is no longer available on the ACCA website.

Economic Value Added (EVA)

Cash earnings* before interest but after tax	x
Imputed charge for the capital consumed.	(x)
Economic Value Added	x

*After "economic depreciation" which measures the true fall in the value of assets each year through wear and tear and obsolescence

Imputed capital charge = capital employed × weighted average cost of capital (WACC)

Capital employed = shareholders' funds + non-current liabilities (i.e. equity + debt).

EVA attempts to convert financial accounting profit to "economic profit" to show any surplus returns above the minimum required by providers of finance.

Financial accounting profit does not deal well with finance costs, in fact totally ignoring equity costs. Managers may wrongly believe that financial accounting profit indicates satisfactory performance.

EVA is a similar concept to residual income, a performance measure you may have seen in earlier studies.

Economic Value Added is sometimes referred to as EVA®. EVA® is the registered trademark of Stern Stewart and Co who have done much to popularise and implement this measure of residual income.

Advantages of EVA

- ✓ It makes the cost of capital visible to managers.
- ✓ It supports the NPV approach to decision making.

Disadvantages of EVA

- ✗ Projects with good NPVs may show poor Economic Value Added in earlier years and thus be rejected by managers with a short-term time horizon.
- ✗ Validity of EVA® adjustments (Stern Stewart and Co suggest up to 164 adjustments to financial accounting profits to arrive at economic profit.)
- ✗ Understatement of the capital base in the service sector where the main capital may be human capital which is not measured on the balance sheet.

Market Value Added (MVA)

= Present Value of Economic Value Added
= Project NPV
= Increase in value of equity (i.e. shareholders' wealth)

Book value of capital employed + MVA = Market value of capital employed

Shareholder Value Added (SVA)

Shareholder Value Added involves calculating the present value of the projected future "free cash flows" of the business. Any increase in this present value should result in an equivalent increase in market value added and thus increased shareholder wealth.

Different definitions of free cash flow exist but for calculating SVA it represents the cash available to shareholders, which in principle could be paid out as dividend or used for share repurchases. This is known as free cash flow to equity. The present value of this free cash flow (discounted at the cost of equity) should equal the current equity market capitalisation of the business, and any changes in this present value (less any shareholder funds subscribed during the period) represents SVA.

If debt interest and principal payments are excluded from the free cash flow (known as free cash flow to the firm) then the present value would be calculated at the WACC. This is because this version of free cash flow represents a return to both equity and debt holders. The resultant present value would then represent the value of debt plus equity in the company. The value of equity could be calculated by subtracting the market value of debt.

The full article can be found at
http://www.accaglobal.com/uk/en/student/exam-support-resources/professional-exams-study-resources/p4/examiners-reports.html

Section A – compulsory 50-mark question

Part (a) asked candidates to discuss a company's acquisition strategies of risk diversification and pursuing under-valued companies. The company in the scenario was *privately* held and in this case a diversification strategy through acquisitions may be valid. Some candidates confused systematic and unsystematic risks.

Many candidates discussed potential synergy benefits in relation to acquiring under-valued companies but few discussed the attributes necessary for the strategy to work.

Part (b) asked why the company was being forced to sell one of its existing subsidiaries before pursuing further acquisitions. Many candidates recognised that there was concern about monopolistic powers and why selling the subsidiary would reduce these concerns.

In part (c)(i) many candidates made a reasonable attempt at determining the initial equity values of an acquirer and target firm but few were then able to calculate the potential gain to each of the two companies.

Part (c)(ii) asked for the value of a project, both with and without an embedded real option to subsequently abandon it through sale to third party.

A surprising number of candidates used the cost of equity as the discount rate instead of a risk-adjusted weighted average cost of capital.

The majority of candidates found it difficult to determine the expected value of the project based on conditional probabilities, despite a recent article appearing on this topic.

Many candidates tried to apply the Black-Scholes model to value of the real option even though no standard deviation figure was provided. Some candidates, incorrectly, assumed that a probability figure was a standard deviation figure.

Part (c)(iii) required evaluation of the benefits of combining the two firms but few candidates went beyond repeating their answers from parts (c)(i) and (c)(ii). There were many easy marks to gain by discussing the assumptions made but many candidates failed to do this.

Many candidates found the calculations in this question difficult and appeared to spend too much time on them. This created pressure to complete the discursive requirements very quickly, the structure of the report was often unsatisfactory and the professional marks were lost.

EXAMINER'S REPORT – DECEMBER 2014

Section B – choice of 2 from 3 25-mark questions

Question 2

Part (a) asked candidates to use traded options and over-the-counter swaps to hedge the cost of borrowing against interest rate fluctuations. Most candidates correctly identified that put options were required although some candidates could not calculate the number of contracts required. Many candidates attempted to calculate the unexpired basis even though it was provided in the question.

A number of candidates did not undertake detailed calculations using both strike prices options but instead provided justification of choosing one over the other. Full credit was given where the choice was justified.

Many candidates found the calculations related to swaps more difficult. Some did not identify the comparative advantage correctly and therefore chose the wrong type of borrowing initially.

In many cases, the discussion and recommendation were not presented in detail or well structured. Hence many candidates did not gain many discursive marks related to part (a).

Part (b) asked candidates to discuss how a centralised treasury department would increase value for the company and reasons for decentralising the treasury department.

Part (c) asked candidates to discuss the key differences between a Salam contract and futures contracts. Some candidates gave little more than a description of Islamic finance and what is forbidden under it, with very little on futures contracts. Better answers considered futures contracts in detail and used the information provided in the question on Salam contracts to construct a good discussion.

Question 3

Part (a) asked candidates to discuss the aims of a free trade area and the benefits to the company of operating within such an area. Common errors included confusing a free-trade area with other types of international organisations, focussing too narrowly on just one aspect of a free-trade area and not considering the benefits to the company or discussing the Euro currency. Part (b) asked candidates to compute the IRR, MIRR and VAR of a project and compare them to the figures provided for another project. The NPV of both projects was also provided in the questions.

The majority of candidates provided corrects calculations for the IRR and MIRR, and discussed the implications from the results well. However some candidates calculated several NPVs in order to estimate the IRR which resulted in wasting valuable time.

Many candidates could not calculate the VAR over the project's life and could not explain what the figure meant.

Very few candidates could link the risk aspect measured by VAR to the risk-return discussion of which project to accept.

Part (c) required discussion of the legal risk of undertaking a project outside the company's current trading area. Answers included a general discussion of risks, instead of legal risks in particular, and many omitted a discussion on risk mitigation strategies.

Question 4

Part (a) asked candidates to discuss the advantages and drawbacks of the EVA^{TM} technique. Some candidates framed the same aspect both as an advantage and as a drawback and therefore and others just stated what the EVA^{TM} was rather than discussing the advantages and drawbacks.

Part (b) asked candidates to calculate the company's EVA^{TM} over two years. Many answers applied finance costs incorrectly when calculating taxation and many calculated the capital employed incorrectly. The marking team accepted average or year-end capital employed figures, although opening figures are considered to be more accurate.

Part (c) required further performance evaluation and many candidates correctly identified that gearing was an issue and the proposal to finance the new investment using debt was probably not wise.

Fewer candidates discussed the investment strategy of the company, which focused on the less profitable construction business, to the detriment of the more profitable hospitals and biomedical business. Very few candidates linked the flawed investment strategy to the company's share price performance.

Many answers to part (c) were presented unsatisfactorily. Often answers would calculate a ratio or trend and immediately attempt to analyse it. A better approach is to calculate and tabulate the ratios and trends, and analyse the performance holistically.

Conclusion

A sustained study, over a long period of time, is an essential pre-requisite for success in paper P4. On the exam day it is critical to use the reading and planning time appropriately, then produce neat and well-structured answers which specifically address the requirements and relate to the scenario.

ANALYSIS OF PAST EXAMS

Topic	June 2015	Dec 2014	June 2014	Dec 2013	June 2013	Dec 2012	June 2012	Dec 2011
Business valuation	B	A	B	B	A, B	A, B	A	
M&As		A	B	B	B	B	A	
Forex hedging			A		B	A		
Performance evaluation/EVA™	B	B						
MIRR		B					B	
VAR		B					B	
Euro crisis						B		
Cost of capital calculations		A	B		A	A	B	A
Role of free trade areas/WTO		B		A				
Stock exchange listing					A		B	
Corporate governance, environmental and ethical issues	A		A		A			B
Treasury centralisation/decentralisation		B						
Islamic finance		B		B				
Capital reconstructions					A			

©2015 DeVry/Becker Educational Development Corp. All rights reserved.

ANALYSIS OF PAST EXAMS

Topic	June 2015	Dec 2014	June 2014	Dec 2013	June 2013	Dec 2012	June 2012	Dec 2011
Unbundling/divestment	B			B		A		
Capital rationing						B		
Dark pools	B							
APV			B		A			A
Overseas project appraisal	A			A	A		B	A
Dividend capacity/policy					B			
Interest rate derivatives	B	B	A	B			B	A
Domestic project appraisal		A	B			B		
Black Scholes/ROPT			B	A			A	
Multilateral netting					B			
MBO/MBI	B							B
Delta hedging/Greeks			B	B	B			
Bond valuation/duration			A					B

A – In section A of the exam (i.e. as whole or part of a compulsory scenario-based question)

B – In section B of the exam (i.e. as an optional question)

EXAM TECHNIQUE

Do not try to pass the exam by only performing calculations (or by only making discussion). Balance your time according to the mark allocations.

In calculations show your workings and write your assumptions. In an exam at this level there will rarely be a unique "correct" answer, particularly in subjective areas such as business valuation. The examiner and his marking team are flexible – just show them that you can make a reasonable attempt and they will be sympathetic – perfection is not expected.

When asked to comment on your calculations do not be afraid to do so even if you think your calculations contain errors – you can still get maximum marks for comments.

If you could not perform the required calculation then write an assumed result and comment on that.

Structure your comments using sub-headings and bullet points (but write a full sentence after each bullet). If asked for a report format then obviously be more formal (i.e. introduction, main body, conclusion and appendix) but bullet points can still be used within the report for clarity.

Do not throw away the professional marks available in section A.

Give real life examples where appropriate to support your comments – extra marks may be awarded. Examples can be taken from your home country.

Generous marks are often available in early requirements for performing relatively straightforward calculations (e.g. estimating WACC) or basic discussion (e.g. suggesting various sources of debt finance). Later requirements may ask for something very complex – but only for a few marks.

If you pick up the easier marks where available and at least make an attempt at the more complex requirements then you should be awarded a pass.

The examiner has identified the following common weaknesses in candidates' performance:

✗ A lack of knowledge of the entire syllabus – including current issues. This can be put right through a strategy of sustained study, instead of last minute intensive preparation and trying to spot questions and/or topic areas;

✗ Poor time management – some candidates spend far too long on some questions and this puts them under time pressure to finish the remaining questions. Proper time management between questions and parts of questions is essential;

- Illegible handwriting and poor layout of answers – it is very important to plan and structure answers properly. Good, clear handwriting is essential. Adopting these good practices will also enable candidates to get the majority of the professional marks available;

- Not learning lessons from examiner's reports – many of the same comments are made repeatedly in the examiner reports.

The examiner has stated that excellent answers contain the following elements:

1. Knowledge and understanding of the entire P4 syllabus – last minute intensive study, question spotting and relying on hints is a strategy that is unlikely to yield success.

2. Application of knowledge and understanding to the scenario given in each question – weaker answers make general comments rather than being specific to the scenario.

3. A balanced answer for all the parts of each question, whether the part required discussion or calculations or both – make sure that you can answer all requirements of a section B question before selecting it.

4. Effective time management – weaker candidates spend too long in section A and then rush through section B. For example in June 2013 some candidates had difficulty obtaining a relevant discount rate in question 1 (a, i). In this case, they should take a sensible guess and move to part (a, ii). Candidates will always get credit if their approach is correct, even though an earlier error results in an incorrect final answer.

5. Legible, well presented and well-structured answers will also enable candidates to get the majority of the professional marks available. Well-structured answers also enable candidates to manage their time more effectively.

6. Do a quick check; does your numerical answer make sense? For example if your calculated cost of equity is below the cost of debt then you have made an error. If you cannot find the source of your error then at least state that you realise an error has been made.

EXAM TECHNIQUE

ABOUT BECKER PROFESSIONAL EDUCATION

Becker Professional Education provides a single destination for candidates and professionals looking to advance their careers and achieve success in:

- Accounting
- International Financial Reporting
- Project Management
- Continuing Professional Education
- Healthcare

For more information on how Becker Professional Education can support you in your career, visit www.becker.com.

Substantially derived from content reviewed by ACCA's examining team

Lightning Source UK Ltd.
Milton Keynes UK
UKOW06f0908260116

267129UK00013B/95/P